The Seven Principles
of
SUCCESSFUL
MARRIAGE

The Seven Principles of Successful Marriage
Copyright © 2022 by Hilaire Louis Jean

Published in the United States of America

ISBN   Paperback: 978-1-959165-82-8
ISBN   eBook: 978-1-959165-83-5

All rights reserved. No part of this publication may be reproduced, stored in a retrieval system or transmitted in any way by any means, electronic, mechanical, photocopy, recording or otherwise without the prior permission of the author except as provided by USA copyright law.

The opinions expressed by the author are not necessarily those of ReadersMagnet, LLC.

ReadersMagnet, LLC
10620 Treena Street, Suite 230 | San Diego, California, 92131 USA
1.619. 354. 2643 | www.readersmagnet.com

Book design copyright © 2022 by ReadersMagnet, LLC. All rights reserved.

Cover design by Kent Gabutin
Interior design by Daniel Lopez

The Seven Principles
of
SUCCESSFUL MARRIAGE

Hilaire Louis Jean

ReadersMagnet, LLC

CONTENTS

INTRODUCTION ix
THE MEANING OF MARRIAGE xi
TRUST xv
FAITHFULNESS, FIDELITY, AND SEX xvi
FORGIVENESS xviii
RESPECT xix
LOVE xxi
SUMMARY xxiii

CHAPTER 1:   TRUST 1
CHAPTER 2:   FAITHFULNESS 11
CHAPTER 3:   FIDELITY 25
CHAPTER 4:   SEX 30
CHAPTER 5:   FORGIVENESS 36
CHAPTER 6:   RESPECT 46
CHAPTER 7:   LOVE 55
CHAPTER 8:   BUILDING A FAMILY 68
CHAPTER 9:   THOSE WHO OPPOSE MARRIAGE 81
CHAPTER 10: A SUPPORTIVE COUPLE 93
CHAPTER 11: THE LITTLE THINGS MARRIED
              COUPLES SHOULD KNOW 103
CHAPTER 12: FAMILY WORK-LIFE BALANCE 112

CONCLUSION 125
REFERENCE LIST 133
ABOUT THE AUTHOR 145

Dedication

With great pleasure I dedicate *The Seven Principles of a Successful Marriage* to my dearly beloved wife, Yanick. From the time our Lord Jesus brought us together as husband and wife, you have stood by my side as my best friend. Even though we have had some difficult times, Jesus has always been in control of our lives together. You are my greatest supporter and the most significant partner I have in ministry. You have been my companion and counselor; you have allowed me to answer the call of God Almighty and travel across the globe for the cause of the gospel.

To my beautiful daughter, Rebecca, and my son in-law, Asthelin Fils-Aime, who always help me get things done on time.

To my two loving sons, Marc Hilaire and Marvin E. Louis Jean, who always helped when I had to work late at night.

To my five loving grandchildren: Monae, Akiem, Damoni Donje, Ruth Izabella and Adriana who always stayed quite when I had to work in my home office.

To the memory of my mother, who is now with the Lord, the late Metelia Louis Jean; and to my father, Ilermeau Louis Jean, who is ninety-five years old and always praying for me and my family.

To all the members of the Church of God Prince of Peace in Miami, Florida, for their love, devotion, and prayers. I would also like to thank Pastor Charles Bellerive, Pastor Josette Vallon, Evangelist Pierre Richard Jeannith, and the deacons' board of Church of God Prince of Peace for their prayers.

Introduction

The Seven Principles of a Successful Marriage

I was born into a poor Christian family in a small city in the mountains of Miragoane, Haiti. Life was very challenging. My late mother married my father when she was sixteen years old and my father was nineteen years old. They did not have the opportunity to go to school because their parents could not afford the expense. Yet my parents loved each other and their children. Although they did not have much money, they built a successful marriage in accordance with the Word of God.

As the third eldest child in my family, I learned many excellent lessons from my parents' marriage. My father always treated my mother with kindness, gentleness, and love. The Bible tells husbands to love their wives with God's love, "even as Christ also loved the church, and gave Himself for it" (Ephesians 5:25 KJV). In turn, my mother respected my father, who was a deacon in his local church. As a child, I observed that they always prayed and asked God for guidance in everything they pursued.

Moreover, my parents always treated all of their children with respect. They instilled in us a sense of self-esteem and hope. They consistently gave us love and support, disciplining us when necessary. I enjoyed the way I was treated by my parents, and I am proud to pass on their strategies to my own children, especially the emphasis on spending time together as a family. Family bonding is more necessary today than ever before, and parents facilitate it by instilling the basic values of hope, self-esteem, discipline, and love.

The Meaning of Marriage

The concept of marriage carries multiple meanings with varying nuances across different cultures and religions. In the United States, marriage is a legal contract signed by a couple in accordance with the state in which they live. Spiritually, it is a covenant between two people to love and cherish each other for life.

Marriage is a relationship between a man and a woman intended by God to be a monogamous relationship, intended to be a permanent bond in which many needs are satisfied—the need to love and to be loved, the need for deep friendship, for sharing, for companionship, for sexual satisfaction, for children, the need to escape loneliness. Marriage ought to be a bond of love, reflecting the love Christ has for His people, a bond of sacrificial love where husband and wife have become one, one flesh, a unity. (Wright and Roberts 1997, 6).

From a biblical perspective, companionship is a crucial component of marriage. When God observed Adam's loneliness in the Garden of Eden, He created Eve as a companion (Genesis 2:20). Companionship is vital in bringing spouses together and helping them achieve closeness and intimacy. "The emphasis is on the family as a unity of interacting persons that shapes the personality development of its members and is itself adaptable to change" (Burgess and Locke 1945, 800).

According to Genesis 2:18, the first marriage was celebrated by God. As the creator of the universe, He performed the first wedding ceremony in the Garden of Eden. "The Lord God said, 'It is not good for the man to be alone. I will make a helper suitable for him" (Genesis 2:18 NIV). According to pastor and author Michael Pearl, "Marriage is the commitment to cleave to one's mate in an unconditional, irrevocable choice of his or her will. Marriage is God's permanent, sacred covenant and should not be taken lightly; marriage is God's laboratory for the perfecting of the human race" (2012, 9). Likewise, *Nelson's Minister's Manual* states that "marriage is commended in the Scriptures to be honorable among all, and therefore is not by any to be entered into unadvisedly or lightly but reverently, discreetly, advisedly, soberly, and with the fear of God" (15). Therefore, understanding and respecting marriage is essential to Christian practice. Specifically, a couple should establish their union under a canopy supported by seven pillars, or principles: (1) trust, (2) faithfulness, (3) fidelity, (4) sex, (5) forgiveness, (6) respect, and (7) love. If couples commit to these principles, they will realize a strong, positive marriage.

While companionship is a cornerstone of marriage, it is not the only determinant of a couple's happiness. "I feel very strongly that marriage is not a higher calling than the single state. Happy indeed are those people, married or single, who have discovered that happiness is not found in marriage, but in a right relationship with God" (Kendall and Jones 2005, 14). If a couple desires to build a successful marriage and a loving life together, they must first invite Jesus into their marriage and relationship.

Jesus is always interested in marriage, but it is up to individuals to welcome Jesus into their marriages. For example, in the New Testament, Jesus and His disciples were invited to a marriage in Cana of Galilee. The Bible explains that during the wedding reception, the family ran out of wine (John 2:2–3). In the Jewish wedding tradition, running out of wine in the middle of the reception was a serious breach of etiquette and a problem that did not bode well for the marriage. Fortunately, Jesus was at the event and, wanting the couple to have a happy marriage, performed a miracle by turning water into wine. It is a wise decision for people to invite Jesus as the first guest to their marriage.

Marriage should be a reflection of the bond of love that Christ has for His people. It is a bond of sacrificial love by which a husband and wife unite and become one flesh (Genesis 2:18–24). The concept of "one flesh" comes from the account in Genesis 2:21–24 when God created Eve by taking a rib from Adam's side as he slept and fashioning it into a woman. Adam recognized that Eve was part of him; they were, in fact, "one flesh." The term implies that just as the human body is one entity that cannot be divided and still survive, so too did God intend the marriage relationship to be unbreakable. There are no longer two entities (two individuals), but now there is one entity (a married couple). Let's consider a number of aspects to this new union.

First, marriage is two people working together to fulfill both their own and their mate's needs (including sexual needs) in the way God intended. According to Michael Pearl, "Marriage is designed to meet the need of intimacy and love for each other. Therefore, when a man doesn't give love to his wife, he doesn't give love to his home, his children, or himself. Just as Eve was literally created from Adam's rib, a wife is figuratively her husband's rib, and man with a broken rib next to his heart is a crippled man" (2012, 120). Consequently, marriage, if it is to succeed, must be a commitment in which there is no holding back of anything.

Second, many couples desire to cleave to each other as one. However, before committing fully to another human being, a potential spouse must have a clear understanding of what holy matrimony entails. Marriage enables individuals to share a joyful life together, yet no marriage comes without its obstacles. For example, in some cases, husbands and wives have been raised in different cultures and societies. Accordingly, they may hold different values and worldviews. Regardless of the circumstances, a couple must build their marriage with honesty and sincerity, the latter of which is demonstrated by speaking and expressing feelings genuinely. It is imperative that couples establish shared principles before they declare their wedding vows. "One of the saddest reasons a marriage dies is that neither spouse recognizes its value until it is too late" (Mack and Blankenhorn 2001, 463).

Finally, marriage is a pledge of mutual fidelity in all areas. It is a partnership of "mutual subordination and servanthood" (Wright and Roberts 1997, 27). For this reason, the Creator spoke to the husband and wife at the same time. God did not intend for individuals to lose their identities in marriage, but rather for them to cleave unto each other in a deep and profound way. When couples live together as a married couple, it is a beautiful communion and experience in which they learn to help each other freely. Ultimately, this sacrament leads to the formation of a family.

Children are an important element of the family and thrive from their parents' love and attention. The parents must ensure that their children's basic psychological and physiological needs are met. By sharing their love and values with their children, parents can assure that their offspring will lead happy, successful lives. Therefore, the seven principles of marriage—trust, faithfulness, fidelity, sex, forgiveness, love, and respect—extend beyond the couple to their children. As long as a couple adheres to these principles consistently, they will establish a prosperous marriage and family. Let's take a brief look at these foundational pillars.

Trust

Trust is founded on honesty and integrity and is an important pillar of marriage.

Interpersonal trust is an aspect of close relationships which has been virtually ignored in social scientific research despite its importance as perceived by intimate partners and several family theorists. . . . Analyses of human relations suggest that "trust" is an integral feature of such relationships. Trust is generally defined as a belief by a person in the integrity of another individual. (Larzelere and Huston 1980, 94)

Trust means that both partners will not harm the other intentionally. It also signifies that spouses can rely on each other at all times with full confidence.

When spouses marry, they agree to become one flesh as long as they both shall live. The seemingly simple words "I do" can be deceptively complex, however. In addition to moving into a new home or community, recently married couples also begin a new chapter of their lives. This journey is founded upon shared values, hopes, and dreams. Married couples must further be able to commit to and confide in each other. In order to build a life together, they must be able to trust each other fully. Such mutual trust sets the stage for a beautiful marriage.

Faithfulness, Fidelity, and Sex

Faithfulness is the concept of remaining unfailingly loyal to someone else and putting that loyalty into consistent practice, regardless of extenuating circumstances. Faithfulness is not just about loyalty; it is also allegiance. It is the reason partners stay together, no matter what happens, no matter the hurts, the physical ailments, the financial issues, or any number of the other things that can tear a marriage apart. It's being present in the heart, mind, body, and spirit of the marriage. It's sensing when your spouse is tired and doing something special for them. It's taking a burden off your partner when they are struggling. It is sharing in the trials and joys of the day-to-day living that marriage brings. In truth, faithfulness brings the greatest spiritual dimension into the marriage.

Some women and men do not sleep around with others, but they do talk harshly and disrespectfully about their spouses to friends or coworkers. Adhering to the letter of the marriage contract, they think they are being faithful to their partners, but in reality, they are not. If spouses are truly faithful to each other, then they will refuse to disparage their partners by complaining about them or talking about them in unflattering ways; instead, they will be careful to consider their partners' needs. Faithful spouses will see their partners through eyes of love, respect, trust, and forgiveness. Without these traits, a marriage cannot demonstrate faithfulness.

Faithfulness between spouses, both sexually and otherwise, allows individuals to become more intimate with each other. The Bible explains, "He that is faithful in that which is least is faithful also in much: and he that is unjust in the least is unjust also in much" (Luke 16:10). Human beings should be faithful to God and to one another. The concept of faithfulness is a very broad one that encompasses a range of actions and behaviors.

Fidelity is an aspect of faithfulness that specifically refers to the loyalty between spouses in the sexual domain. Sex is an important component of marriage because it allows couples to reproduce. God wants married couples to bear children and populate the earth (Genesis 2:24). In this sense, women are of special importance because God gave them the ability to reproduce humankind. The Bible warns against fornication, which applies to sex outside of marriage or unmarried individuals engaging in sexual activities. The apostle Paul says, "To avoid fornication, let every man have his own wife, and let every woman have her own husband" (1 Corinthians 7:2). Paul, in addressing the immorality in the Corinthian church, discussed this topic (1 Corinthians 5:1).

Forgiveness

Sometimes spouses make mistakes and must seek forgiveness from their partners. Humans may falter in any of the principles described above as well as in other areas. Forgiveness is the action or process of being pardoned by another individual. This means that the person who was wronged no longer harbors resentment or ill feelings toward the other (*Webster's New World Dictionary* 2016, 529).

The Bible advocates forgiveness as an important value. For example, in the Lord's Prayer, Jesus says, "Forgive us our debts, as we forgive our debtors" (Matthew 6:12 NIV). In this statement, Jesus demonstrates that forgiving is a mutual need. To avoid divorce in marriage, mutual forgiveness must be ongoing. No one is perfect. Both partners in a marriage must acknowledge their imperfect condition as human beings and be ready to give and to receive forgiveness at all times.

Respect

Forgiveness is related to respect in that partners must have respect for each other if they are to pardon each other's mistakes. In marriage, respect requires that partners hold each other in high esteem and show honor to each other. Doubt typically exists in the absence of such mutual admiration. In speaking to women, Eggerichs says, "There are many ways to show your husband respect. Just look for ways to appreciate his desire to protect and provide, especially when things aren't going too well for him" (Eggerichs 2004, 210).

If partners do not completely trust each other, they will withhold their deepest, most intimate thoughts and musings. God, however, created and designed marriage to be the most intimate of all human relationships. "We are going to share life intellectually, socially, emotionally, spiritually and physically and we are going to share life to such a degree that it can be said of us, that we become one" (Chapman 2003, 35). Privileged insights are reserved for those who refuse to deceive, but emotional separation drives a wedge between two individuals. When spouses share respect and a deep connection with each other, they know they will always be there for each other.

A relationship based on common appreciation between spouses is one that is solid and not shaken by outside influences. When respect is present, relationships are like the one described in Proverbs 31, where the "husband has full confidence in [his wife] and lacks nothing of value" (Proverbs 31:11 NIV). Valuing a mate means showing appreciation in marriage.

Love

Trust, faithfulness, fidelity, sex, forgiveness, and respect work together to bring love into a marriage. The Bible describes three categories of love: (1) God's love for humanity, (2) man's love for God, and (3) human beings' love for one another. Only if a man loves God first can he truly love his wife, and vice versa. Love unites couples as they feel constant affection and attraction for each other. With love, partners are able to espouse their Christian values and principles as they collaborate to build a strong relationship. "When a Christian has a healthy marriage, the whole world looks bright. When the marriage relationship is empty, it negatively affects all other aspects of life" (Chapman 2003, 2).

Love is an ongoing process that takes time to cultivate, and it generally grows when the couple bears children. Love allows people to feel cared for and protected. When love is unconditional, it is able to overcome even the most trying and difficult circumstances, and the couple's marriage will be stronger than ever.

Summary

Marriage is an important part of Christian life. Created by God, this sacrament does not come without trials and tribulations. However, if a couple's relationship is grounded in shared values and understanding, the marriage will be prosperous.

The aforementioned seven pillars of a successful marriage should be used as guiding principles and focal points in the family. They can also be used as a guide for struggling couples to prevent divorce and facilitate a return to marital happiness. In the following pages, we will explore these seven principles of a successful marriage in greater detail.

Chapter 1: Trust

Marriage is a covenant between two people to love and cherish each other for life. Jesus Himself clearly viewed marriage as a lifelong covenantal relationship (Matthew 19:4–9). On their wedding day, two people stand before a minister and make a covenant. With eyes wide open, they enter into a new stage of their relationship and acknowledge the hard work demanded in committing to undivided and exclusive love. Before they enter into such a lifelong relationship, however, they have to trust each other.

The minute couples get married; their lives are united as one. Therefore, trust must be at the center of their marriage. But what is the meaning of trust? Trust is the "assured reliance on the character, ability, strength, or truth of someone or something." Trust can further be defined as "something committed or entrusted to one to be used or cared for in the interest of another. Trust is a virtue necessary in all relationships, but the trust that Christians have is completely different from that of others.

A husband and wife must be able to trust each other fully in order to enjoy the full benefits of their union and experience the peace that comes from trust. Let's look first at trust in the role of the wife. In order for a marriage to be successful, a wife must be able to trust that her husband will fulfill his role as the head of the house. The apostle Paul writes in Ephesians 5:23–25:

For the husband is the head of the wife as Christ is the head of the church, his body, of which he is the Savior. Now as the church submits to Christ, so also wives should submit to their husbands in everything. Husbands love your wives, just as Christ loved the church and gave himself up for her.

Jesus is the Son of God. To fulfill His role as the head of the church, He paid the price on the cross. As a result, we can trust in His promise of salvation (Luke 23:33–43). Likewise, the man must fulfill his role in the marriage as the head of the house. His wife and children must be able to trust him to fulfill his responsibilities.

In turn, the wife must demonstrate trust in her husband. There are two ways she can do this. The primary way is through her submission to her husband. Submission is defined as the action or fact of accepting or yielding to a superior force or to the will or authority of another person. When a wife submits to her husband, not only is she pleasing him, but she is also obeying the Word of God: "Wives, submit yourselves to your own husbands as you do to the Lord" (Ephesians 5:22 NIV).

The second way a wife exhibits her trust in her husband is through the respect she shows him. The degree to which a wife reveres her husband is the degree to which she reveres her Creator (Pearl 2010, 22). Wives are to respect their husbands, according to the Bible. For example, Sara called her husband, Abraham, "my lord." She knew that Abraham was not her Lord and Savior, but she used the word *lord* as a sign of admiration and great respect for him.

Even as Sara obeyed Abraham, calling him lord: whose daughters ye are, as long as ye do well, and are not afraid with any amazement. Likewise, ye husbands dwell with them according to knowledge, giving honour unto the wife, as unto the weaker vessel, and as being heirs together of the grace of life; that your prayers be not hindered. (1 Peter 3:6–7 KJV)

This is the same way Sara approached her Lord: with reverence.

Just as a wife must know that her husband loves her, so a man must know that his wife respects him in order for their union to reflect the pattern that God intended for married couples to live by.

Submission in Marriage

While many think of submission as yielding to a superior force, there is another definition. The Greek word used for *submission* in Paul's discussion on marriage is *hupotasso*, which has the military meaning of "to arrange [troop divisions] in military fashion under the command of a leader," and the non-military meaning of "a voluntary attitude of giving in, cooperating, assuming responsibility, and carrying a burden" (Ladd, 208). Christian wives are called to this second definition of submission.

A husband is not better or superior to his wife, but he exercises authority over her as the person responsible for answering directly to God. A woman's neglect of her biblical role in marriage creates confusion. For example, Eve's actions in the garden did not show submission to Adam, and as a result, sin entered the world.

"We may eat fruit from the trees in the garden, but God did say, 'You must not eat fruit from the tree that is in the middle of the garden, and you must not touch it, or you will die.'"

"You will not certainly die," the serpent said to the woman. "God knows that when you eat from it your eyes will be opened, and you will be like God, knowing good and evil."

When the woman saw that the fruit of the tree was good for food and pleasing to the eye, and also desirable for gaining wisdom, she took some and ate it. She also gave some to her husband, who was with her, and he ate it. (Genesis 3:2–6 NIV)

Eve assumed the position as the head of the house and negotiated the deal with Satan on behalf of Adam. The biblical position she should have taken was to refer Satan to her husband as the head of the house. This would have left her free of sin. Instead, she usurped her husband's responsibility, negotiated with Satan, and ate the fruit. Worse yet, Eve knew she was not behaving according to God's commands. She disobeyed God's instructions, and she consequently had to suffer the consequences for her behavior. In addition, the Bible says in Romans 6:23 that "the wages of sin is death," and God held Eve accountable for her actions.

Likewise, we see Adam's abrogation of his God-ordained role. In taking cues from his wife rather than investigating the situation with his Lord, with whom he enjoyed direct fellowship, he chose to take on the submissive position, which led to his decision to follow in Eve's footsteps and eat the fruit. Because of his failure to exercise authority, God expelled Adam and Eve from the garden, and sorrow and death became part of their lives. Adam paid for Eve's mistake, and all of mankind paid for Adam's mistake. This illustrates a powerful truth. There is no such thing as a winner and a loser in marriage; there are either two winners or two losers. Ultimately, men are charged with the primary responsibility of seeing that their marriages function as God intended.

The idea of submission in marriage is not limited to the Old Testament. According to Dr. Tony Evans (2010, 25), pastor of Oak Cliff Bible Fellowship, author, and evangelist, there are two concepts of submission and respect in the New Testament. Stated in Ephesians 5:22–33 and 1 Peter 3:1, these two elements walk side by side. First, Paul summarized each individual's responsibility. Later, Peter addressed wives about how to be a blessing to their husbands, saying, "Likewise, ye wives, be in subjection to your own husbands" (1 Peter 3:1 KJV). Peter then added an important description of what respectful submission looks like.

The New International Version of 1 Peter 3:1 reads, "Wives, in the same way submit yourselves to your own husbands so that, if any of them do not believe the word, they may be won over without words by the behavior of their wives." Peter obviously recognized the benefit of a submissive wife in helping lead her husband to salvation. He also recognized the benefit to a believing husband, as he himself traveled with his wife, going out into the world and spreading the faith (1 Corinthians 9:5). One can imagine what life might have been like for him if his wife had not been submissive while they traveled together to preach the Word of God in the presence of unbelievers. It would have been a catastrophe for his ministry.

At this point, it is necessary to reaffirm that submission does not mean weakness. The world's definition of submission is very different from the one encouraged in the Bible. For example, a wife shows submission unto her husband when she allows him to take leadership as the head of the house. His position as leader is biblical (1 Corinthians 11:3).

Christ Himself submitted: "Being found in fashion as a man, He humbled Himself and He became obedient unto death, even the death of the cross" (Philippians 2:8). Jesus was not weak, but He was obedient to His Father. As a result, God was pleased with Him. When Jesus Christ went to the Jordan River and was baptized by John the Baptist, the Holy Spirit descended upon Him in the form of a dove. A voice from heaven declared, "This is my beloved Son, in whom I am well pleased" (Matthew 17:5). Jesus pleased God, and God was happy with this kind of submission. Similarly, when a woman submits to her husband, she is not weak; rather, she is simply trusting God and acting according to the Word of God.

Both men and women were created in the likeness and resemblance of God. Men and women are equal in the eyes of God, but a woman's place in the hierarchy of God is to be submissive to her husband. Christians must remember that submission is from and for God, not man. As Jesus submitted to God, the church submits to Jesus, each husband submits to

Jesus, each woman submits to her husband, and children submit to their parents. "Let the Lord be magnified, who has pleasure in the prosperity of his servant" (Psalm 34:27 KJV). When there is submission in a family, blessing comes down from God to the family.

Obviously, times have changed considerably since Christ walked the earth. However, it is important to remember that submission is not an outdated concept from a time long ago or a culture far away. The Word of God will never change: "Heaven and earth shall pass away, but my words shall not pass away" (Matthew 24:35). Ultimately, it is that Word that we can trust above all else.

One must always remember that Satan is a liar, and it is important to dwell in the Word to fight his schemes. John 10:10 says, "The thief cometh not, but for to steal, and to kill, and to destroy." One can see clearly that the devil visited the Garden of Eden to destroy Adam and Eve's relationship with each other and with God. The devil manipulated Eve's mind and made her believe that the words of God were not to be trusted. Even today, Satan tries to destroy marriages and relationships between people and with God in the same way. Instead of dangling fruit from the Tree of Life, Satan dangles other temptations, like adultery, rebellion, and the belief that we know better than the Word of God. However, God has provided us with a means of protection. "Submit yourselves, then, to God. Resist the devil, and he will flee from you" (James 4:7 NIV).

What Is Trust All About?

Sometimes individuals try to convince themselves that their spouses trust them. But what is trust all about? What does a husband have to do to earn his wife's trust? How can a wife know if her husband really trusts her? What does an individual have to do to regain a spouse's trust after it has been lost? The answers to these questions must come from the Word of God. The Word of God says, "But seek first the kingdom of God and his righteousness, and all these things shall be added to you"

(Matthew 6:33 NIV). The apostle Paul tells us in Romans 14:17 (NIV) that "the kingdom of God is not a matter of eating and drinking, but of righteousness, peace and joy in the Holy Spirit."

The Husband's Role

Paul says, "Whoever loves his wife, loves himself" (Ephesians 5:28). This is true because a wife is a complement to her husband. The Bible does not ask wives to love their husbands, yet God commands husbands to love their wives: "Husbands, love your wives and do not be harsh with them" (Colossians 3:19 NIV). The apostle Paul urged the Colossian men not to be harsh with their wives; after all, no one wants to be treated harshly. To be a suitable husband to his wife, a man must show lovingkindness. How can a husband prove that he loves his wife? Jesus provided a perfect example in the way that He loves His church. In fact, according to Dr. Tony Evans (2010, 26), "The best way that a man is to love his wife is when he becomes her own savior." In other words, does your wife believe that you are her protector? Is your love for her sacrificial? Have you really convinced your wife that you love her as Christ loves His church?

Two verbs to consider are *to love* and *to give*, and these two action verbs go hand in hand. Christ demonstrated His love for the church when He gave His life for it. If a man loves his wife, he will give himself to her. In fact, there will be nothing so big that a man cannot give it to his wife. "Set me as a seal upon thine heart, as a seal upon thine arm: for love is strong as death; jealousy is cruel as the grave: the coals thereof are coals of fire, which hath a most vehement flame" (Song of Solomon 8:6 KJV).

The word *love* is very easy to say, but it needs to be proven through action. One of the likely reasons for the large number of divorces in America is that individuals fail to understand the meaning of marriage before entering into it. They fail to recognize that marriage is giving one's life to someone else.

If a husband says he is willing to give his life to his wife, he must in reality be willing to give everything to her. A husband should not strive to be right all the time or to always have the last word in every situation. Neither spouse can pick what they like while denying what they do not like. Marriage is all-encompassing, and love is necessary to surround and hold everything together, especially when circumstances don't go as expected. Each spouse must work for the good of the other and the whole family.

Unfortunately, humans are selfish by nature. We always seem to put ourselves first. We dream of what our partners will do for us rather than what we can do for them. If our partner does everything the way we want it to be done, we believe that we have a good partner. However, if the partner fails to fulfill even one expectation, then our view of our mate is blemished by this one small mark of imperfection. For this reason, it is important to enter marriage with the belief that it will be a long-term relationship.

One thing to remember is that in marriage, there are mountains as well as valleys. In fact, all of life is filled with both mountains and valleys. During the great moments, it is easy to be happy and think you have a wonderful marriage, because you are surrounded with success. It is easy to remember that God is great. However, it is important to remember the other part of the marriage vows: "For better or for worse, for richer, for poorer, in sickness and in health, to love and to cherish, 'til death us do part" (*Nelson's Minister's Manual* 2003, 17).

Life is not one mountaintop experience after another; there are valleys too. The troubles of life and difficult moments do arrive. Jesus knew that. That's why He said, "I have told you these things, so that in me you may have peace. In this world you will have trouble. But take heart! I have overcome the world" (John 16:33 NIV). Sickness, the death of a loved one, unexpected bills, and the loss of a job are all valleys that many people face. These are the days that the marriage vows ask you to consider. It is important to maintain trust and bear with your spouse's imperfections, especially in times like these.

When my wife and I first fell in love, we were full of joy, laughter, and fun. We never grew tired of seeing each other, we had new projects to do on a daily basis, and our conversations were never finished. Even though we spent hours on the phone, we had enough energy to continue. Before we got married, I used to pick up my fiancée so we could go to church together. We started to pray together because we both wanted the days to pass quickly so we could get married and live together. We had fresh minds, and we renewed our minds in prayer daily, a habit I learned from my parents.

My wife and I were married on Saturday, April 28, 1984, at 6:00 p.m. at Philadelphia Church of God in Little Haiti in Miami, Florida, in a ceremony officiated by Bishop Joseph Sterling. That day our new life began. It was not easy. After we got married, my wife quickly applied for a green card for me, but I still had to wait a year before I received it. It was another six months before I secured a work permit, so I was not able to start working until October 11, 1985. However, despite this difficult time, we were happy. As Proverbs 17:22 says, "A merry heart doeth good like a medicine." A merry heart also makes a healthy and happy marriage.

In addition, we both trusted in God, and we knew for sure God would never abandon us. Trust in God was the key for the success of our marriage. The journey has not always been easy, but God has always been faithful to our family. We strive constantly to keep Him in His proper place in our marriage—at the head of it. "And hope does not put us to shame, because God's love has been poured out into our hearts through the Holy Spirit, who has been given to us" (Romans 5:5 NIV).

A woman must consider how to be a companion to her husband, because God said, "I will make a helper who is just right for him" (Genesis 2:18 NIV). In the same manner, a man must consider how to be a companion to his wife and love her as the Bible says to do. For both spouses, God has said, "It is not good for man [or woman] to be alone" (Genesis 2:18 NIV).

Chapter 2: Faithfulness

When partners are able to trust each other fully, they learn to be faithful to each other. Being faithful is one of the best ways to ensure God's blessings upon the marriage. God Himself is faithful, and He therefore expects faithfulness between spouses and within the family. If a man is unfaithful to his wife, he is unfaithful to himself and cannot please God. "But without faith it is impossible to please him: for he that cometh to God must believe that he is, and that he is a rewarder of them that diligently seek him" (Hebrews 11:6 KJV).

Faithfulness is an important concept throughout the entire Bible, and it is an essential character trait that God wants each of His children to cultivate. The more faithful a married couple is, the more responsibility God can give them in regard to their family (Wiersbe 2007, 10). Being faithful pleases God, and it is a virtue that should be increasing in the life of every married couple. There is one more thing to remember about faithfulness, and it is perhaps even more important: the more faithful we are in this life, the more we will store up treasure in heaven.

Examples of Faithfulness in the Bible

Faithfulness is an important characteristic discussed throughout the Bible. In fact, it is one of the nine qualities listed as the fruit of the Spirit:

"But the fruit of the Spirit is love, joy, peace, forbearance, kindness, goodness, faithfulness, gentleness and self-control. Against such things there is no law" (Galatians 5:22–23 NIV). God holds up many faithful people as examples to follow and shows how their lives were blessed as a result of their faithfulness.

Noah

In Genesis, the Bible describes the condition of the world in Noah's time: "Now the earth was corrupt in God's sight and was full of violence" (Genesis 6:11 ASV). God told Noah to make an ark, saying, "Make thee an ark of gopher wood; rooms shalt thou make in the ark, and shalt pitch it within and without with pitch" (Genesis 6:14 ASV). Noah responded in faith when God asked him to build the ark, despite the seeming ridiculousness of building a ship atop a mountain and far from ports or water. Regardless of the obstacles, Noah's faith in God was very strong; he proved that by obeying the word of God and building the ark. As a result of his faith, he and his family were saved. "God's covenant reflected his love for Noah's response to that love: Noah was a righteous man, blameless among the people of his time, and he walked with God" (Chapman 2003, 18). Noah was faithful.

Abraham

Abraham, too, demonstrated great faithfulness to God. When he was asked to sacrifice his son Isaac, he did not inform his wife Sarah about his plan. That does not mean Abraham was not faithful to Sarah; rather, it shows that Abraham's faith was so great that he believed God would eventually do something greater in regard to his son. He even said to his servants, "Stay here with the donkey while I and the boy go over there. We will worship and then we will come back to you" (Genesis 22:5 NIV). The fact that he told them he and his son would return shows that he believed God would do something. And of course, God provided a ram to sacrifice in the place of Isaac. As a result, Abraham called that place "Jehovah Jireh," or "the Lord will provide" (see Genesis 22:1–14). God blessed Abraham because of his faithfulness, making him the father of a great nation.

Joseph (Son of Israel)

As a teenager, Joseph had many dreams. His dreams, however, incited his brothers to hate him. Furthermore, Genesis 37:3 says, "Now Israel loved Joseph more than any of his other sons, because he had been born to him in his old age; and he made an ornate robe for him" (Genesis 37:3 NIV). This special treatment caused Joseph's brothers to resent him even more, and because of that, they plotted against him. Even though Joseph was sold into slavery, falsely accused, and imprisoned, he never lost faith in God (Genesis 39:1–23). As a result, he was eventually awarded authority that saved his whole family during a famine. He told his brothers, "Now therefore be not grieved, nor angry with yourselves, that ye sold me hither: for God did send me before you to preserve life" (Genesis 45:5). Through Joseph's faithfulness, God sheltered and grew the nation of Israel in Egypt.

Moses

Like the others mentioned above, Moses, too, was faithful. God instructed him to lead the Israelites out of Egypt, through the Red Sea, into the wilderness, and to the Promised Land, but many great dangers lay in their path. However, Moses was faithful, and he was a true believer in God despite all the perils he had faced when still in Egypt. Moses knew that God would not deliver him or His people into the hands of the enemy. By the power of his God, he successfully led all the children of Israel through the Red Sea. Because of his faithfulness, Moses is included in what is known as the Bible's "Hall of Faith":

By faith he left Egypt, not fearing the king's anger; he persevered because he saw him who is invisible. By faith he kept the Passover and the application of blood, so that the destroyer of the firstborn would not touch the firstborn of Israel. By faith the people passed through the Red

Sea as on dry land; but when the Egyptians tried to do so, they were drowned. (Hebrews 11:27–29)

Ruth

Ruth was a faithful servant of the Lord who gave her life for her mother-in-law. In doing so, she violated the law of her country. At that time, if a husband died when his wife was still young, and his mother had no other sons and could not bear more children, the widow was supposed to leave her mother-in-law to find another man to marry. Instead of leaving, Ruth told her mother-in-law, "Don't urge me to leave you or to turn back from you. Where you go I will go, and where you stay I will stay. Your people will be my people and your God my God. Where you die I will die, and there I will be buried. May the Lord deal with me, be it ever so severely, if even death separates you and me" (Ruth 1:16–17 NIV). Ruth faithfully stayed with her mother-in-law, Naomi, after her husband died. She also faithfully followed Naomi's instruction regarding Boaz, and as a result, Ruth blessed her mother-in-law and was grafted into the lineage of Jesus Christ.

David

David was a faithful king who shepherded God's people. Because of his unwavering faith in God, David won a great battle with the giant Goliath. David beheaded Goliath with the giant's own sword. No one at that time believed that David could win the battle against the giant, but David confidently declared, "Though my father and mother forsake me, the Lord will receive me" (Psalm 27:10 NIV). He did not count on anybody but his God, and he was thus successful in the battle.

David continued expressing his confidence in the Lord when he wrote Psalm 27: "The Lord is my light and my salvation; whom shall I fear? The Lord is the stronghold of my life; of whom shall I be afraid? When the wicked advance against me to devour me, it is my enemies and my foes that will stumble and fall" (verses 1–2 NIV). Accordingly, Psalm

27 proves that David had no fear of Goliath or anybody else in his time, because he trusted in the Lord. In Psalm 121:1–2, he so beautifully said, "I will lift up mine eyes unto the hills, from whence cometh my help. My help cometh from the LORD, which made heaven and earth."

Mary and Joseph

It is no surprise that the woman chosen to give birth to Jesus was an example of faithfulness. Even though she endured many hardships (including a long, hard journey while pregnant and having to deliver her baby in a stable), she remained faithful to her husband and to God. She never complained about the difficulties she faced.

In the same way, Joseph, too, was faithful. When he first learned that Mary was with child, he was undoubtedly shocked and hurt. After all, the woman he was supposed to marry was pregnant, and he was not the father (Matthew 1:19). However, when the angel told Joseph the truth about how Mary had become pregnant, he stayed with her. Joseph trusted what the Lord said. Despite the difficulties they encountered, Mary and Joseph was a couple that showed great faithfulness to God and to each other.

Faithfulness in Marriage

Before a couple can even consider faithfulness to each other, they must make sure they are faithful to God in every aspect of their lives. Take, for example, a pastor who had a young couple in his church who were about to marry. One day the pastor's phone rang. The pastor answered and heard the man trying to speak with him while the young lady cried in the background. The young man said, "Pastor, we are about to enter the courtroom to get our marriage license, but I don't like the way my fiancée is talking to me. I don't want to marry her anymore." The pastor asked if he could talk to the man's fiancée, and he agreed. The pastor asked her to explain what was happening.

Without any hesitation, she said, "Pastor, I have two major problems with my fiancé. The first problem I have is that he doesn't want to pay his tithe to God. I have asked him repeatedly, but he says that he doesn't believe in tithing. With that outlook, I don't know where our blessing will come from.

"I also told my fiancé that since I am working and make about $1,100 biweekly, I would like to give my mother, who is a widow in Haiti, about $50 biweekly, and I would like to continue paying my tithe." She continued, "My fiancé says if I talk like that, I am not being submissive."

The pastor asked both of them to come into his office to discuss the situation further. When they arrived, he encouraged the young man to remember that his fiancée was about to become his lifetime blessing. The pastor added that it seemed as if the man would not be able to handle this blessing God had sent his way. He then explained that the woman had not said anything wrong; she had been faithful to God and simply wanted to continue being faithful to God after she said "I do." Furthermore, she had not asked her fiancé to take care of her mother; she merely wished to support and bless her own mother, a poor widow living in a poor country, with a $50 biweekly stipend from her own earnings. The young lady's mother was a priority in her life. It was important for her to honor her mother by contributing to her income.

In regard to the tithe, the young lady said, "Pastor, in my family, we didn't have much to give to the Lord, but we always gave our tithes." In her family, they believed tithing was their hope, and that by giving back to the Lord, they would welcome His blessings into their lives. The young woman wanted to make it clear to her fiancé that she would continue giving because she did not want to close the door to God's blessings on them after their wedding.

After much discussion, the couple prayed together, and they reached an agreement to work and live according to the Word of God. The Bible explains in Malachi 3:10, "Bring ye all the tithes into the storehouse, that there may be meat in mine house, and prove me now herewith, saith the LORD of hosts, if I will not open you the windows of heaven, and pour you out a blessing, that there shall not be room enough to receive it."

Faithfulness is likewise emphasized in the New Testament. Through His parables, Jesus taught the importance of being faithful, drawing attention to the fact that His disciples are stewards and must be faithful with the resources they have been entrusted with by God. Luke 16:10 (NIV) says, "Whoever can be trusted with very little can also be trusted with much, and whoever is dishonest with very little will also be dishonest with much."

Married couples will grow in faithfulness as they invest generous portions of their money and time into the work of God. They should not allow the desire for money or possessions to control them. As the apostle Paul, in his first letter to his young disciple Timothy, said, "For the love of money is the root of all evil: which while some coveted after, they have erred from the faith, and pierced themselves through with many sorrows" (1 Timothy 6:10). This verse is often misquoted as "money is the root of all evil," but that is incorrect. Money is not the root of all evil; rather, the love of money is the root of all evil.

Finances are often a source of turmoil in marriage. It is important for a couple to realize that focusing too much on money can lead to sin and sorrow, tearing their relationship apart. However, when husband and wife are faithful to God's commands, they will also be faithful and loving to each other.

In the famous chapter on love, 1 Corinthians 13 says:

Love is patient, love is kind. It does not envy, it does not boast, it is not proud. It does not dishonor others, it is not self-seeking, it is not easily angered, and it keeps no record of wrongs. Love does not delight in evil but rejoices with the truth. It always protects, always trusts, always hopes, and always perseveres. (Verses 4–7 NIV)

Love is patient, not only with one's spouse, but also with everything else. One of the reasons that people do not always see God's love is because they ignore the meaning of love and forget that it is patient. Another reason many people do not see God's promises come to pass is because they become discouraged and forget that long-suffering is a part of love. It is easy to become frustrated in marriage. However, just because one does not see anything happening does not mean that God is not working. Hebrews 11:1 says, "Faith is the substance of things hoped for, the evidence of things not seen." Faithfulness and patience work together.

Certainly, God is faithful in all things. Most people dream about getting married and having a family. Some couples hope for a child or wish to start a business. Others desire to move to a safer neighborhood or buy a new house. All of these are excellent dreams, and couples may feel that God has given them these desires. Often, however, when goals seem to take too long to transpire and individuals experience disappointments, they become negative and start thinking they will never attain their goals. They may also start to take matters into their own hands. Even some of the heroes of faith listed in Hebrews 11 struggled with this.

For instance, God's promise of descendants and a great nation to Abram was wonderful, but it had to begin with at least one heir. Many years passed between the time Abram left Haran and the birth of his son Isaac. Abram questioned God many times, asking when his promised son would be born. Abram even tried to hurry things along by fathering a child with his wife's maidservant, Hagar. However, all Abram's impatience brought about was more strain on his marriage. Abram had to learn to be patient and wait for God's perfect timing. God did not tell Abram how long he was going to have to wait for Isaac, so Abram had to trust God to lead him one day at a time.

When God sends a trial to us, our first response is usually, "Why, Lord?" and then, "Why me?" Right away, we want God to give us explanations. Of course, we know that God has reasons for sending tests, perhaps to purify our faith (1 Peter 1:6–9), perfect our character (James

1:1–4), or even to protect us from sin (2 Corinthians 12:7–10), but we fail to see how these things apply to us. The fact that we ask our Father for explanations suggests that we may not know ourselves as we should or God as we should. Abraham heard God's word and immediately obeyed it by faith. "Isaac shall thy seed be called" (Genesis 21:12). Abraham believed that even if God allowed him to slay his son, he could raise Isaac from the dead (Heb. 11:17–19). Faith does not demand explanations; faith rests on promises. (Wiersbe 2007, 87).

A couple committed to living together for life is not immune from experiencing problems or disappointments. In those times, it is important to maintain faith in God. He can work out good in any situation, no matter how difficult. Romans 8:28 (NIV) says it clearly: "And we know that God causes all things to work together for good to those who love God, to those who are called according to his purpose." Though it is difficult to do so, a couple should pray to and worship the Lord, even in their suffering. As the apostle Paul says:

Rejoice in the Lord always: and again I say, rejoice. Let your moderation be known unto all men. The Lord is at hand. Be careful for nothing; but in everything by prayer and supplication with thanksgiving let your requests be made known unto God. And the peace of God, which passes all understanding, shall keep your hearts and minds through Christ Jesus. (Philippians 4:4–7)

Faith in the Lord can turn things around from negative to positive, even when situations are beyond human control. Jesus told His disciples, "With man this is impossible, but with God all things are possible" (Matthew 19:26 NIV).

The Understanding of Faithfulness

The public level of marriage is based on the public image, or how others view and discuss the couple. The public image portrays the relationship between the couple to the rest of the world. For example, the couple's friends or coworkers may view the marriage a certain way, but it may not be totally accurate. Most married couples do their best to behave accordingly when they are in public, but their interactions may be perceived differently by individuals in various areas of their lives. For instance, a close friend may know that the couple is struggling with infertility, while a coworker may think that everything is fine.

The second level of faithfulness can be observed in the home when there is nobody else around. This level reflects the true relationship between husband and wife. The husband should comply with the Word of God by loving his wife as the Bible tells him to do. Likewise, a wife should submit to her husband as the Bible instructs. The level of faithfulness between husband and wife should be evident to their children as well. Children should learn from their parents what a strong and faithful marriage looks like. They should be able to look at their parents and learn how to pray and rejoice, even in hardship. When a husband and a wife are faithful to each other, the blessing of the Lord will come down to their house and bring joy and peace of mind to the family for generations to come.

If you fully obey the LORD your God and carefully follow all his commands I give you today, the LORD your God will set you high above all the nations on earth. All these blessings will come on you and accompany you if you obey the LORD your God: You will be blessed in the city and blessed in the country. The fruit of your womb will be blessed, and the crops of your land and the young of your livestock—the calves of your herds and the lambs of your flocks. Your basket and your kneading trough will be blessed. You will be blessed when you come in and blessed when you go out. (Deuteronomy 28:1–2 NIV)

A faithful couple will make healthy decisions because their lives agree, and those decisions and actions will set the tone for the rest of their lives.

The third and deepest level of faithfulness is the inner level of marriage. Often in marriage, partners hide emotions and thoughts from each other. However, what goes unsaid about a spouse or is only felt deep inside indicates the real health or illness of the marriage. Speaker and author Nancy Groom (2000, 12) explains this by saying, "Sometimes, the unseen dynamic in the relationship is hidden even from the marriage partners themselves. For whatever reasons, one or both may be unable or unwilling to look honestly at true feelings about each other."

When a man is faithful to his wife at this inner level, it shows that he is fully committed to her and their marriage. He desires to love and cherish his wife faithfully. He will remain emotionally committed and share his deepest feelings with her and no one else. In addition, he will demonstrate sacrificial love, relinquishing his wants and desires to serve her needs. If this inner level of faithfulness is strong, it will make the other levels of the marriage strong as well. "The wise woman builds her house, but with her own hands the foolish one tears hers down" (Proverbs 14:1 NIV).

In the Old Testament, we read that the children of Israel were unfaithful to God. For instance:

They made a calf in Horeb and worshipped the molten image. Thus they changed their glory into the similitude of an ox that eateth grass. They forgat God their saviour, which had done great things in Egypt; wondrous works in the land of Ham, and terrible things by the Red Sea. Therefore he said that he would destroy them, had not Moses his chosen stood before him in the breach, to turn away his wrath, lest he should destroy them. (Psalm 106:19–23 KJV)

Conversely, the less faithfulness there is in a marriage, the more fragile it is. Relationships must be protected from the attacks of Satan.

Contract Marriage and Covenant Marriage

According to Gary Chapman, there are two types of marriages. The first one is a contract marriage. In a contract, or legal, marriage, "If one party does not live up to the contract, then legal actions force them to do so or to end the marriage with an equitable settlement" (Chapman 2003, 7). Most, if not all, marriages today are contract marriages. Even if a legal contract is not actually signed, there is at least a spoken agreement in place. After all, marriage itself means joining lives; thus, everything must be done accordingly, and each spouse must live up to the contract.

Dr. Chapman says that most married couples make numerous contracts with each other on a daily basis (2003, 7). An example of such a contract is "if you will take the children to school, I will clean the house and make dinner tonight." These informal contracts become part of a couple's day-to-day life and are, in fact, essential in married life. There would be no successful marriage without respected contracts between both parties. With an agreement in place, the couple will have to support each other one way or another. Like with any other kind of contract, both parties must keep it and be faithful to their promises; otherwise, the relationship can be dissolved.

According to Gary Chapman, a successful marriage requires a lifetime contract, which can be either written or verbal. In the Garden of Eden, a marriage contract existed between Adam and Eve. It was a verbal contract between the two of them, and God was the performer of the marriage and the witness of the contract. God is also the witness of the Christian marriage today. "For where two or three gather in my name, there am I with them" (Matthew 18:20 NIV).

The second type of marriage is a covenant marriage. A covenant is defined as a legal means to establishing kinship between two previously unrelated parties. "Covenants are initiated for the benefit of the other person" (Chapman 2003, 13). David had a covenant with Jonathan, King Saul's son: "From that day King Saul kept David with him in the palace and he did not allow him to return back to his father's house. And Jonathan made a covenant with David because he loved him as himself" (1 Samuel 18:2–4 ASV). While a contract is established for a limited period of time or a set number of years, a covenant is a lifelong commitment. A contract expires at the end of the predetermined period; covenants do not have similar expiration dates. In other words, a covenant is for a lifetime.

While this does not mean that individuals who get married outside of the church necessarily view marriage as a short-term commitment, it does point to the devotion and commitment with which a Christian should approach marriage. Christian marriage is covenant marriage because it goes beyond an earthly partnership. According to Christian educator and counselor H. Norman Wright, the marriage covenant is a commitment involving three individuals: a husband, a wife, and Jesus Christ. He describes it by saying, "A Christian marriage is a total commitment of two people to the person of Jesus Christ and to one another. It is a commitment in which there is no holding back of anything. Marriage is a pledge of mutual fidelity in all areas. It is a partnership of mutual subordination and servanthood" (2012, 25–26).

Faithfulness is critical in both contract marriage and covenant marriage. "So long as we both shall live" and "till death do us part" are two promises often made regarding faithfulness in Christian marriage (Chapman 2003, 8). Under God's authority, loving one's spouse is a faithful action to God. That is also why the apostle Paul says, "Love your wife as Christ loved the church," and "if you love your wife, you love yourself" (Ephesians 5:25, 28 NIV).

Christ's love for the church is unlimited and unrestricted. Likewise, a man should exhibit the same kind of unlimited and unrestricted love and devotion for his wife. A devoted spouse becomes an enthusiastic and faithful partner. God commands, "Finally, be ye all of one mind, having compassion one of another, love as brethren, be pitiful, and be courteous" (1 Peter 3:8 KJV). "In my survey of wives, 85 percent of them said the most important prayer a husband could pray was that he would become the man, husband, and head of the home God wanted him to be. This is the most important place for a man to begin praying" (Omartian 2001, 32). It's definitely something well worth praying about. Whenever a couple is faithful to God and to each other, God will send His blessings upon them.

Divorce Is Not the Solution

God is faithful, and He always keeps his promises. He never lets His people down. Even though there may be times in marriage when things look very dark and the situation seems out of control, divorce is not the solution. Unfortunately, many people, including Christians, do indeed view divorce as the solution. According to the US Census Bureau, the divorce rate in America is nearly 50 percent, and while statistics vary as to the rate of divorce among Christians, the numbers are generally similar and even greater in some places. Many of these people end their marriages only to discover they now have severe, long-term problems.

God discourages divorce. Jesus says in Matthew 19:9 (NIV), "Because of your hardness of heart Moses permitted you to divorce your wives; but from the beginning it has not been this way. I tell you that anyone who divorces his wife, except for sexual immorality, and marries another woman commits adultery." Being faithful, even in a difficult or troubled marriage, is not always easy, but God will reward those who seek after Him and follow His commands. He has said, "If you listen carefully to the voice of the Lord your God and do what is right in his eyes, if you pay attention to his commands and keep all his decrees, I will not bring on you any of the diseases I brought on the Egyptians, for I am the Lord, who heals you" (Exodus 15:26 NIV).

In addition, God will help His people as they strive to obey Him. Hebrews 13:6 (KJV) states, "So that we may boldly say, The Lord is my helper, and I will not fear what man shall do unto me." Without couples practicing patience and understanding, divorce will continue to happen on a daily basis. However, if a couple is committed to remaining faithful to each other, God will honor them and help strengthen their marriage.

Chapter 3: Fidelity

There are three types of fidelity: (1) physical fidelity, (2) mental fidelity, and (3) emotional fidelity. One definition of fidelity is a husband's and wife's faithfulness to each other in their sexual relationship. However, Kenneth W. Matheson (2009), professor in the School of Social Work at Brigham Young University, defines fidelity as "complete commitment, trust, and respect between husband and wife."

Therefore, in the case of Christian marriage, fidelity relates to much more than physical intimacy. True intimacy between husband and wife is about the giving and receiving of everything—physical, mental, and emotional. Many people understand that the Bible instructs that sexual relationships outside of marriage are adulterous, but they fail to realize that the Bible also teaches that fidelity stems from the mind. Jesus said, "But I tell you that anyone who looks at a woman lustfully has already committed adultery with her in her heart" (Matthew 5:28). Consequently, a Christian couple must be careful to guard not only their bodies, but also their minds and emotions. If a spouse develops a relationship that compromises spiritual fidelity, that spouse should humbly take the necessary action to reinstate the marital relationship.

Physical Fidelity

Physical infidelity is adultery, which most people are familiar with. As early as the Ten Commandments, God commanded His people not to commit adultery (Exodus 20:14). In the Old Testament, the term *adultery* referred to voluntary sexual intercourse of a man, either single or married, with a married woman who was not his wife. Under the Law, adultery was punishable by death: "If a man commits adultery with another man's wife—with the wife of his neighbor—both the adulterer and the adulteress are to be put to death" (Leviticus 20:10 NIV). The seventh commandment was primarily a safeguard for the home and the marriage bond rather than a general commandment of moral purity.

God is faithful in His relationship with His people: "And I will betroth thee unto me forever; yea, I will betroth thee unto me in righteousness, and in judgment, and in lovingkindness, and in mercies. I will even betroth thee unto me in faithfulness: and thou shalt know the Lord" (Hosea 2:19–20 KJV). In Hebrews 13:4 (NIV), Paul echoes the faithfulness sentiment that couples are called to when he says, "Marriage should be honored by all, and the marriage bed kept pure, for God will judge the adulterer and all the sexually immoral." Therefore, physical fidelity is not only critical to achieving a successful marriage, but it also keeps believers in right standing before God. "Or do you not know that wrongdoers will not inherit the kingdom of God? Do not be deceived: Neither the sexually immoral nor idolaters nor adulterers . . . will inherit the kingdom of God" (1 Corinthians 6:9–10 NIV).

Likewise, abstaining from sexual relations before marriage is very important for a successful marriage. The Bible calls sexual relations before marriage "fornication." Fornication is a sin, and all sins are an affront to God Almighty, who is holy. However, some sins are specifically mentioned as an abomination to God. Jesus reminded the Pharisees that after a couple is married, "they are no more twain, but one flesh. What therefore God hath joined together, let no man put asunder" (Matthew 19:6 NIV). Paul tells the Corinthian church to "flee from sexual immorality. All other sins a person commits are outside the body, but whoever sins sexually, sins against their own body" (1 Corinthians 6:18 NIV).

Faithfulness in marriage must start even before the marriage vows are exchanged. A man cannot be unfaithful to his fiancée now and think that after they get married, he will be faithful to his wife. Keeping the marriage bed pure, as Paul commands in Hebrews, requires self-control in all stages of life, not just after the vows are exchanged. Later, Paul told the Corinthians, "Each man should have sexual relations with his own wife and each woman with her own husband" (1 Corinthians 7:1–2 NIV). He went on to also address the unmarried, saying, "If they cannot control themselves, they should marry, for it is better to marry than to burn with passion" (1 Corinthians 7:9 NIV). Clearly, Christians must commit to fidelity to their future spouses regardless of where they are in the relationship. Even if a couple has plans to get married, they should wait until after the wedding to consummate their relationship.

Mental Fidelity

The story of King David and Bathsheba, Uriah's wife, is a great example of how dangerous lust can be.

One evening David got up from his bed and walked around on the roof of the palace. From the roof he saw a woman bathing. The woman was very beautiful, and David sent someone to find out about her. The man said, "She is Bathsheba, the daughter of Eliam and the wife of Uriah the Hittite." Then David sent messengers to get her. She came to him, and he slept with her. (Now she was purifying herself from her monthly uncleanness.) Then she went back home. The woman conceived and sent word to David, saying, "I am pregnant." (2 Samuel 11:1–3 NIV)

Ultimately, this incident led to Uriah's death, under the direction of David. However, the adultery with Bathsheba was not David's first sin in this situation, but rather, it was his lust for her. That lust then led to the other sins of adultery and murder. Although this example may seem extreme, it illustrates the importance of exercising mental fidelity in a marriage. A married couple should entertain sexual thoughts only about each other. Of course, just as in David's time, there will always be attractive people around. However, lusting after a person and admiring beauty are two different things. As Paul warned, "Abstain from all appearance of evil" (1 Thessalonians 2:22).

Today's society is filled with many temptations. Pornography is easily accessed online, while magazines with scantily clad women and erotic romance novels are available at many local convenience stores. Even television commercials and store displays use sexual images to grab viewers' attention. Both women and men are targeted with these images. The apostle Paul offers this solution: "Finally, brothers and sisters, whatever is true, whatever is noble, whatever is right, whatever is pure, whatever is lovely, whatever is admirable—if anything is excellent or praiseworthy—think about such things" (Philippians 4:8). By focusing their thoughts on the things of God and on their own spouse, Christians can avoid many of the temptations of this world and maintain mental fidelity in their marriage.

Emotional Fidelity

Emotions are a very important component of marital fidelity. Married couples can have friends of the opposite gender, but within limits. Becoming emotionally close to someone other than a spouse is dangerous because it can lead to mental and physical infidelity. When Jesus taught His followers how to pray, He said, "And lead us not into temptation, but deliver us from evil" (Matthew 6:13). The phrase "lead us not into temptation" in the Lord's Prayer means not to be in a position to fall into temptation. By staying out of compromising situations, a person has less opportunity to succumb to temptation.

In addition, spending intimate time with one's spouse allows for a stronger marital bond, which makes illicit entanglements with others less tempting. This is why Paul told the Corinthians, "Defraud ye not one the other, except it be by consent for a time, that ye may give yourselves unto fasting and prayer" (1 Corinthians 7:5 KJV). According to this verse, husband and wife may mutually consent to abstain from sexual relations for a certain period of time in order to pray, but they should come back together as soon as the period is ended.(1 Cor. 7). By spending intimate time together, a husband and wife fill each other's emotional, mental, and physical needs, and there is less room to fall into temptation.

The fidelity of each spouse will ultimately complete the foundation of the marriage. If partners remain sincere and faithful to each other, they will construct a strong foundation built on Christ that will not crack under the pressures of life. Therefore, it is important to guard against any hint of physical, mental, or emotional infidelity if one wishes to have a strong and happy marriage. A marriage can be placed in a precarious situation if one spouse forms a relationship with someone outside the marriage and begins to choose the company of that person or frequently shares personal information with that person rather than with the spouse. The problem can occur with either husband or wife.

Fidelity in marriage includes refraining from physical contact with others, but that is not all. Fidelity also means complete commitment, trust, and respect between husband and wife. Inappropriate interactions with other people erode fidelity. According to Dr. Kenneth Matheson (2009, 2), "Fidelity means spouses don't share the sensitive parts of their hearts that should be exclusively reserved for their spouse only. Sharing their hearts in this way can divide and deprive their marriages of something special and unique."

Chapter 4: Sex

According to Michael Pearl (2012, 19), sex is a small need compared to the need of having a soul mate. Couples thinking about having sex before their marriage should think about how the two of them are going to cleave to each other as one for life (Genesis 2:24). In 1 Corinthians 7:4, the Bible says, "The wife has not power of her own body, but the husband: and likewise also the husband has not power of his own body, but the wife." This verse refers to the fact that the husband and the wife belong to each other, meaning neither has the right to refuse reasonable sexual requests.

Sex has the power to unite two people. Many cultures have a public wedding ceremony, but sexual intercourse is a private consummation. It's important to note that couples who communicate well with each other and share activities are often more active sexually. Paul says in the book of Ephesians, "Always be humble and gentle. Be patient with each other, making allowance for each other's faults because of love" (Ephesians 4:2). "Sex is designated to be a unique expression of our commitment to each other for a lifetime" (Chapman 2010, 184). It's unlike anything else in a marriage relationship; it is incomparable, unequal, and irreplaceable.

Sex is the act that leads to procreation between a man and a woman. Sexual intercourse is also the manner through which human beings experience and express their emotions and feelings for one another. Although it is impossible to create a baby without an egg and a sperm, people have sex for many different reasons besides procreation.

Just as trust and faithfulness contribute to a successful marriage, so too does sex pave the way for marital happiness. In the beginning, Adam was not looking for sex; rather, he was looking for a soul mate. "Your wife is more than your sex toy; she is the other half of your humanity" (Pearl 2012, 49).

The Bible tells us that our bodies are the temple of the Holy Spirit: "Do you not know that your bodies are temples of the Holy Spirit, who is in you, whom you have received from God? You are not your own; you were bought at a price. Therefore honor God with your bodies" (1 Corinthians 6:19–20 NIV). Although fornication is a widely accepted aspect of Western culture—even among Christians—it is critical to understand that it is not part of God's design for healthy relationships and renders far-reaching consequences that can carry over into marriage.

"Neither let us commit fornication, as some of them committed, and fell in one day three and twenty thousand" (1 Corinthians 10:8). This is a clear warning against immorality. The Bible does not authorize anyone to commit fornication, even with a fiancé or future wife. The critical thing to remember is that there is nothing inherently wrong with sex or with the sex act itself. The key is that it must done in the proper context—marriage. God created the sex act and designed it to be a pleasurable experience for a married couple to share.

Sadly, however, many young men and women jump from one partner to another, looking for sex and satisfaction. What many ultimately discover is that sex alone cannot bring deep satisfaction. If it could, King Solomon would have been satisfied, since he had seven hundred wives and three hundred concubines.

Intimacy

Nothing produces loneliness like a lack of intimacy. According to Bishop T. D. Jakes (2011, 367), pastor of the Potter's House in Dallas, Texas, "A wedding is not completed until the union is consummated. Also, the marriage will have no substance if the couple has no regular intimacy." The sexual relationship is a part of marriage. Therefore, after marriage, the married couple will not live well if sex is excluded. Other things may be good, but nothing can be compared to or is more powerful than a man's sexual relationship with his wife. Nothing has the same ability to create intimacy as does the sexual relationship. Although intimacy takes many forms for different people, there is a certain level of intimacy in a marriage that can be attained only in the active presence of a sexual relationship.

Some individuals believe that they do not need to be committed to each other to have sex, that "casual sex" is permissible. Casual sex does not involve intimacy because there is no commitment in it. Generally, individuals who engage in such behavior are simply seeking physical pleasure without the attachment of emotions or deep feelings. On the other hand, when a married couple shares sexual intimacy, they share an emotional bond with each other, and the focus is on making the partner feel cherished and cared for.

Emotional intimacy is established when two people can comfortably share their feelings with each other or empathize with each other. It is demonstrated when each tries to understand and be aware of the other person's feelings. According to Schaefer and Olson (1981, 32), "Intimacy is a process and an experience which is the outcome of the disclosure of intimate topics and sharing of intimate experience. Furthermore, intimacy is defined as a multifaceted interpersonal dimension that describes the quality of marital relationships."

Additionally, "Intimate relationships seem to buffer people from the pathogenic effects of stress. In the face of stressful life events, people who have intimate relationships have fewer stress-related symptoms, faster recoveries from illness, a lower probability of relapse or recurrence than those who do not have intimate relationships" (Prager 1997, 1).

As stated before, sex is a gift from God to man and woman. God gave us the ability to enjoy sex, not only so that we could create a family and bear children, but also as a way for us to bond and experience intimacy. God wants us to experience fulfilling, joyful sexual relations with the person to whom we are married—and only with him or her.

Flee from sexual immorality. All other sins a person commits are outside the body, but whoever sins sexually, sins against their own body. Do you not know that your bodies are temples of the Holy Spirit, who is in you, whom you have received from God? You are not your own; you were bought at a price. Therefore honor God with your bodies. (1 Corinthians 6:18–20 NIV)

Types of Marriage

According to Pastors Mark and Grace Driscoll (2012, 53), there are three types of marriage relationships: (1) back-to-back, (2) shoulder-to-shoulder, and (3) face-to-face. "A back-to-back marriage is one in which a couple has turned their backs on each other" (32). A back-to-back marriage will not last because the Bible says that in order to be married, a man and a woman must become one flesh (Genesis 2:24). In a back-to-back marriage, the couple lives separately and does not work together (32). According to Genesis 2:24, a back-to-back marriage is not suitable for having a successful marriage.

Second, "a shoulder-to shoulder marriage is a marriage in which the couple works together on tasks and projects, such as keeping the home, raising the kids, growing the business, and serving the church" (32). In a shoulder-to shoulder marriage, a couple cares for each other and depends on each other in order to achieve a successful marriage.

Third, "the face-to-face marriage is a marriage in which, in addition to the shoulder-to-shoulder marriage, the couple gets a lot of face-to-face time for conversation, friendship, and intimacy" (32). In a face-to-face marriage, a couple spends a lot of time together in order to promote intimacy. "Women's friendships tend to be face to face and built around intimate conversation" (33) and this is the type of relationship a husband and wife should strive to develop.

A heart-to-heart marriage is a marriage in which the couple sticks together at all times. It is a big mistake for couples to invest most of their time into work or business, putting the marriage lower on their list of priorities and leaving their spouse vulnerable. Paul emphasized this very concept: "Do not deprive each other except perhaps by mutual consent and for a time, so that you may devote yourselves to prayer. Then come together again so that Satan will not tempt you because of your lack of self-control" (1 Corinthians 7:5 NIV).

Though this is speaking of sexual union, it also applies to other areas of the marriage that foster true intimacy. "A friendship with an enjoyable spouse can make a world of difference—someone who knows how to have a good time, relax, go on an adventure, or just toss it all to the side for a holy diversion. Any couples who hope to exit this life together still holding hands must be friends who have fun along the way and laugh a lot" (Driscoll and Driscoll 2012, 35). In many cases, however, husbands and wives do not have many opportunities to converse. By putting away distractions like technology, friends, or business partners, a couple can reconnect and form a true heart-to-heart connection.

Issues with Sex in a Marriage

It seems that sex is the guide to functioning well within a marriage. Regardless of how close a couple is, nothing has more power to devastate marital intimacy than sexual infidelity. It is good for a man to have a wife, and also for a woman to have a husband (1 Corinthians 7:2). However, marriage is not a place for anyone to stand for their own rights, elevating their own needs above their partner's. Marriage is a decision to serve the other partner, whether in bed or outside the bedroom.

God created one man, and from that man He took one rib and formed a woman. God's ideal is for each man to have one wife and for each woman to have one husband. As a married couple, "the husband should fulfill his marital duty to his wife, and likewise the wife to her husband" (1 Corinthians 7:3 NIV).

Marriage is important because it was created by God: "And the Lord God said, It is not good that the man should be alone; I will make him an help meet for him" (Genesis 2:18 KJV). From the beginning, marriage was part of God's program, but Satan actively works against it. Satan is the enemy of marriage; his plan is to destroy it and, by extension, one's body and children.

There is a simple step couples can take to strengthen their marriage bond. If marriage partners would relate to each other with an attitude of service, there would be fewer divorces in America and a larger number of successful marriages. And it all begins with forgiveness.

Chapter 5: Forgiveness

Forgiveness is the action or process of forgiving or being forgiven by someone. Understanding forgiveness is central to understanding marriage. Marriage should not be taken lightly, since according to Genesis, God instituted marriage to create families, bear children, and alleviate loneliness (Genesis 2:18).

Before two people decide to unite their lives as one, they must possess a clear understanding of what matrimony entails. Furthermore, couples who desire to meld their lives together must realize that they are from different families, and sometimes they are from different countries, speak different languages, and grew up in different cultures. In these cases, building a marriage on honesty and sincerity is even more critical because overcoming differences requires patience.

It is imperative that married couples establish certain principles in the early stages of their marriage. Forgiveness is one such principle, and it is essential for family life. Let's take a moment to look at the origins of this important element in a successful marriage.

God hates sin. He was not happy when Adam and Eve fell into sin in the Garden of Eden. However, despite their outright disobedience, He still clothed them (Genesis 3:21), an act of mercy that symbolized His forgiveness (Kendall and Jones 2005, 86). In the New Testament, Jesus demonstrated mercy for the woman caught in adultery by forgiving her, although He did not approve of what she had done. He told her clearly, "Leave your life of sin and do not sin again" (John 18:11 NIV).

God is a God of amnesty and forgiveness. This is the key to having the power to release anger and bring joy in its place. Forgiveness must be an active, present act. It cannot be in the past, and it cannot be in the future; it always has to be in the present tense. It is a decision that must be practiced on a daily basis. For example, you cannot forgive a partner today and decide not to forgive tomorrow. That would reap the same result as someone who was eating food and drinking water today deciding to stop eating and drinking tomorrow. It just wouldn't work.

Again, forgiveness must be practiced daily. To enjoy a successful marriage, both husband and wife must dwell in forgiveness "'til death do us part." "Forgiveness is a normal demand in a Christian family" (Swaggart 2006, 65). "Likewise, before a man and woman get married, they need to be ready and understand the meaning of marriage; and how to forgive each other" (Kendall and Jones 2005, 4).

Avoiding Divorce

Unforgiveness and misunderstanding are key factors that lead to divorce. In the Lord's Prayer, Jesus says, "Forgive us our debts, as we forgive our debtors" (Matthew 6:12). Forgiveness is a mutual need. "In order to avoid divorce, mutual forgiveness must be ongoing in the family" (Worthington and DiBlasio 1990, 219). No one is perfect. "All have sinned and fallen short of the glory of God" (Romans 3:23). Just as God forgives people without approving of their sins, we must learn that forgiving others does not mean we approve of their wrongdoing. According to the Old and New Testaments, this is the way God deals with each one of us.

Misunderstandings and extreme expectations among couples are major causes for divorce (Genesis 2:24). What causes fights and quarrels among partners? The apostle James answers:

Don't they come from your desires that battle within you? You desire but do not have, so you kill. You covet but you cannot get what you want, so you quarrel and fight. You do not have because you do not ask God. When you ask, you do not receive, because you ask with wrong motives, that you may spend what you get on your pleasures. (James 4:1–3 NIV)

When couples go down the road of misunderstanding, unforgiveness, and unrealistic expectations, divorce is often the sad result. Divorce, separation of children from their parents, and custody battles in the courts of law all lead to pain and devastation.

Forgiveness must be exercised with steadfast love. Paul commanded husbands to love their wives (Ephesians 5:25) and challenged wives to learn how to love their husbands (Titus 2:4). According to Chapman (2003, 19), steadfast love is a choice. According to Kendall and Jones (2005, 52), we choose our attitudes toward our spouses.

It is important to note the difference between forgiveness and reconciliation. Depending on the offense, reconciliation may not look the same in every circumstance. Reconciliation demands the participation of both the offended and the offender. The offended may forgive the offender but may not want to see or talk to the offender again. In other instances, one of the parties involved may have passed away since the time of the offense (Kendall and Jones 2005, 23).

In marriage, reconciliation implies a restoration of the married couple after a quarrel. Likewise, when a husband and wife completely forgive each other, reconciliation should take place immediately. However, the relationship may not always be restored to the level it was before. The bitterness and desire to punish the other partner may be gone, but the wish to restore things to the way they were may not be strong at the same time. It will require time, patience, and much prayer to heal.

A married couple should be careful to avoid entertaining even the idea of divorce. A conversation took place between Jesus and the apostle Peter about forgiveness. "Peter came to Jesus and asked, 'Lord, how many times shall I forgive my brother or sister who sins against me? Up to seven times?' Jesus answered, 'I tell you, not seven times, but seventy times seven times'" (Matthew 18:21 NIV). Forgiveness like this does not come easily, unless one looks at it from a spiritual perspective.

Forgiveness is the key to avoiding divorce in the family. People must learn to forgive each other; otherwise, even churchgoing couples will end up seeking divorce in a court of law. According to Chapman (2010, 56), Divorce is a lack of preparation before getting engaged to be married, and also the failure to learn the skills of working together as a team. Therefore, for your marriage to be successful and mutually beneficial, you must engage in practical communication before the marriage takes place (Chapman 2010, 23). The great philosopher Aristotle said, in the context of human relationships, "To love is to wish good to someone" (Pangle 2003, 283). Likewise, you must make sure you truly love a person before you actually enter into the marriage. The best way to know that you love someone is when the two of you spend time together and are in constant communication.

Impact of Divorce on Children

It seems that the idea of divorce is an assumption held by many people today. For example, many couples sign a prenuptial contract before getting married, which implies that one or both parties may feel that they will not necessarily remain married for life.

It is not very difficult to find someone who has been divorced, but the impact of divorce on children is often overlooked. Nonetheless, the children of divorce will pay the consequences one way or another.

Children need to have present both of their parents, the mother and the father, to be well taken care of. Both parents are necessary to teach and guide their children to do the right thing.

Findings from a ten-year follow-up of 38 youngsters now 16 to 18 years old, whose parents divorced during the children's early latency, suggest that separation from families and the transition into young adulthood are burdened by fear of disappointment in love relationships, lowered expectations, and a sense of powerlessness. A need for the father, especially among boys, appears to burgeon at middle and late adolescence. (Wallerstein 1987, 199)

Children love to be around both parents; it is a sin to push a child to take sides between the mother and the father. Immediately after a divorce, the courts place children with whichever parent has been awarded custody, making an already insecure child even more insecure. Children, however, look to both parents for support and encouragement throughout childhood and during adolescence. A solid foundation of trust is necessary in order to encourage them to share their critical developmental concerns and to foster openness in the parent-child relationship. Children learn to trust themselves when they receive instruction from trustworthy parents and develop a sense of confidence under their parents' compassionate guidance. Under these circumstances, children will learn to function independently and with increased efficiency. Divorce, however, disrupts the entire process.

Children also learn forgiveness from their parents. Refusing to divorce represents an opportunity to model Christlike forgiveness to the children in a family. Forgiveness must be a focal point in the family, although it is never easy. However, we have the example of Jesus and others in the Bible to help us.

Jesus as the Model of Forgiveness

Jesus suffered may terrible forms of physical abuse leading up to His crucifixion. One of the first horrors inflicted upon Him was a scourging. The word *scourged* is translated from the Greek word *fragello* (Renner 2003, 255). According to Renner (2003, 259), it was one of the most horrific words used in the ancient world. An understanding of scourging is important so that we can see what Jesus endured before He was taken to be crucified.

The Romans were experts in scourging (Renner 2003, 259). After the decision was made to scourge Jesus, He was first stripped completely naked. His entire flesh was open and uncovered, in accordance with Roman law, in order to fully receive the beating from the torturer's whip (Renner 2003, 259). Furthermore, Jesus was then bound to a two-foot-high scourging post. His hands were tied over his head to a metal ring, and His wrists were securely shackled to the metal ring to restrain His body from movement. In this locked position, Jesus could not wiggle or move, preventing Him from avoiding any of the lashes being laid across His back. In spite of all this, Jesus still forgave, saying as He hung on the cross, "Father forgive them, for they know not what they do" (Luke 23:34 KJV).

Examples of Biblical Forgiveness

In the Old Testament, Joseph forgave his brothers, even after they sold him into slavery for thirty pieces of silver. His brothers, jealous because of the attention he received from their father, hated him so much that they planned to kill him; but ultimately, they sold him into slavery. This deep-seated hatred began early in the lives of Joseph and his brothers. Joseph was Jacob's favorite child, and he showed this when he gave Joseph alone a colorful robe. According to Genesis 37:3, "Jacob loved Joseph more than all his children because he was the son of his old age."

In addition to being his father's favorite, Joseph was blessed with wonderful, significant dreams. This caused his brothers to hate him even more. They were afraid that he might rule over them one day, as he did in one of the dreams (Genesis 37:4).

The account of Joseph's forgiveness of his brothers is described later in Genesis when Joseph said to his brothers, "Now therefore be not grieved, nor angry with yourselves, that ye sold me hither: for God did send me before you to preserve life" (Genesis 45:5). According to evangelist Jimmy Swaggart (2006, 45, 14), Joseph's heart was right with God and with his brothers. He impressed upon them that God had taken him out of a pit and placed him upon a throne.

Joseph did not hold any of his brothers accountable for their cruel actions against him. When they showed up in Egypt, they were looking for forgiveness, not knowing Joseph had granted it to them long ago. The brothers feared that after the death of their father, Joseph would bring them to justice, but he did not intend to do that. "And Joseph said unto them, Fear not: for am I in the place of God? But as for you, you thought evil against me, but God meant it unto good, to bring to pass, as it is this day, to save much people alive" (Genesis 50:18–19).

In addition to forgiving his brothers, Joseph forgave Potiphar's wife after she falsely accused him of rape when he refused to commit adultery with her. When we do something good, we usually expect that God will bless us for being obedient to the Word of God. In this case, however, Joseph did the right thing but reaped imprisonment. Despite the imprisonment, Joseph forgave the woman for her false accusation.

Sometime later while still in prison, he again had to forgive someone who did him wrong. After interpreting the dream of Pharaoh's butler, or cupbearer, he asked him, when he secured his freedom, to remember that Joseph was still in prison for a false accusation (Genesis 40:1). However, the butler, when freed just as Joseph said he would be, forgot all about Joseph. Joseph remained a forgotten man until the king of Egypt had a dream that no one else could interpret. Then one of the officers remembered that Joseph could interpret dreams, and this led to his release from prison and eventual promotion in Pharaoh's court (Genesis 41:11–13). During all this time, Joseph forgave those who offended him.

How to Forgive: A Case for Forgiveness

Biblical forgiveness requires extending forgiveness even if the offender does not ask for it or recognize his need for it. For example, "Then Peter came to Jesus and asked, 'Lord, how many times shall I forgive my brother or sister who sins against me? Up to seven times?' Jesus answered, 'I tell you, not seven times, but seventy-seven times'" (Matthew 18:21–22 NIV). In this statement, Jesus makes forgiveness unconditional.

Forgiveness is not easy because it is not natural. It is human nature to hold onto situations in which our egos, authority, or pride is challenged or hurt. However, God calls us to something better. Numbers 14:19 states, "Please pardon the iniquity of this people according to the greatness of your steadfast love, just as you have forgiven this people from Egypt until now." This indicates that the foundation of forgiveness is love—love for others and love for God that encourages us to follow His example and commandment to love our neighbor as ourselves (Matthew 22:39).

Forgiveness of another person does not mean that the offender should not or will not pay the penalty for the crime or wrongdoing committed. However, it important to recognize that it is not our responsibility to exact justice for wrongdoing; that responsibility lies with God. Many verses in the Bible attest to God's ability to exact vengeance on those who do wrong. Psalm 18:47 describes the Lord as "the God who gave me vengeance and subdued peoples under me." Isaiah 35:4 says, "Say to those who have an anxious heart, 'Be strong; fear not! Behold, your God will come with vengeance, with the recompense of God. He will come and save you'" (Isaiah 35:4). Perhaps most revealing is the Lord's commandment to the Israelites in Leviticus, where He stated, "You shall not take vengeance or bear a grudge against the sons of your own people, but you shall love your neighbor as yourself; I am the Lord" (Leviticus 19:18). Forgiveness releases a person from being tied to the pain and the hurt another has caused. It is not optional—it is not simply a good thing to do or a nice gesture to make. Forgiveness is a commandment.

Many people have difficulty admitting wrongdoing and asking for forgiveness. In marriage, admitting wrongdoing and seeking forgiveness can be especially difficult because of the intimate nature of the relationship. If you happen to do something wrong against your spouse, the best thing to do is to repent and ask for forgiveness (Connelly 2005, 21). Forgiveness is critical in a marriage relationship, for without forgiveness, every little slight, whether intentional or unintentional, is elevated to the status of a "make or break" situation. The anxiety this breeds undermines the security needed to maintain a happy, healthy relationship with one's spouse.

In Psalm 32, David beautifully described how he felt after committing a transgression and receiving forgiveness for it: "Blessed is the one whose transgressions are forgiven, whose sins are covered. Blessed is the one whose sin the Lord does not count against them and in whose spirit is no deceit" (Psalm 32:1–2 NIV). This psalm is talking about David's sin with Bathsheba and the subsequent murder of her husband, Uriah (2 Samuel 12). Despite the horrendous nature of David's sin, God still forgave him—totally and unconditionally. When God forgives somebody, that person is truly forgiven. The only thing we have to do to experience this wonderful gift is to confess our sins and ask for God's forgiveness.

According to Jesus, all men need forgiveness (Matthew 6:12). Forgiveness is letting go of the need for revenge and releasing negative thoughts of bitterness and resentment. If you are a parent, you can provide a wonderful model for your children by forgiving. If they observe your reconciliation with friends or family members who have wronged you, perhaps they will learn not to harbor resentment over the ways in which you may have disappointed them. If you are not a parent, forgiveness is still an extremely valuable skill to have. All men alternatively must learn how to forgive others to receive forgiveness from God. (Ponton 2007, 5)

Forgiveness is important in helping us maintain healthy relationships. It allows us to display love for one another and love for ourselves. Forgiveness brings peace, as it allows us to leave the past behind and embrace the future.

Chapter 6: Respect

Respect is defined as "a feeling of deep admiration for someone or something elicited by their abilities, qualities, or achievements." In addition, respect is also defined as to show polite regard by visiting or presenting oneself (*Merriam-Webster's* 2016, 1143). Respect in a marriage is essential, but there is a difference in how husbands and wives perceive the need.

According to Dr. Emerson Eggerichs (2004, 6):

Wives are made to love, want to love, and expect love. Many husbands fail to deliver. Husbands are made to be respected, want respect, and expect respect. Many wives fail to deliver. The result is that five out of ten marriages land in divorce court (and that includes evangelical Christians).

Scripture supports this, with Paul clearly saying that wives need love and husbands need respect (Ephesians 5:33). Learning how to show respect before marriage is the foundation for establishing respect within marriage. Without establishing beforehand a firm foundation of respect, a couple should not proceed into marriage.

Marriage works for those who have the will for it. Marriage gives to those who give to it. Be prepared to make huge, sometimes unfairly huge, contributions into the common pot of your marriage—freely, generously, joyously, continually, and never measuring what your partner puts in. (Ortlund 1985, 16)

That holds true for showing respect in the marriage relationship.

Respectful Communication in Marriage

Respectful communication is the mortar that holds a relationship together and allows each person to accept the other person's point of view. In marriage, it is important that both partners feel that their perspectives and suggestions are valued. Respect in communication is not automatic; it requires an active effort. Like everything else in a marriage, communication should not be one-sided. If one partner dominates all the conversations, offers all the ideas, and wields most of the control or influence, this will impede effective communication and negatively impact the ability to maintain a respectful dynamic. Both partners should be invested and actively engaged in promoting respect through effective communication.

The study of communication as a vital facet of the family processes is receiving increasing prominence in the field of family relations. Many authorities contend that good communication is the key to family interaction and the lifeblood of the mental relationship. (Bienvenu 1970, 26)

Spouses, therefore, must make an effort to be open with each other. This is a critical component of establishing and maintaining healthy communication. One aspect of openness is defined as not keeping secrets. While it is not expected that individuals lose their identities or share every single detail of their lives, past, present, and future, the expectation is that those things that are important and critical are shared between the partners, and that there is not an active spirit of keeping secrets. A marriage is a partnership, and if one party has more information than the other, the playing field is not equal.

"Interestingly enough, scientific research confirms that love and respect are the foundation of a successful marriage" (Eggerichs 2004, 35). "Marriages that make it have two people who can accept imperfections and differences; they have learned how to influence one another in positive ways and bring out the best in each other. They've learned what can be changed and what cannot. Personality types and characteristics won't change; behavioral habits certainly can" (Wright and Roberts 1997, 23).

Love and Respect Are Essential for Marriage

Like forgiveness, respect is a crucial value married couples must embrace. It signifies a feeling of deep admiration for someone or something, elicited by abilities or achievements. Respect also denotes kindness and goodness toward others. Respect is both given and received; we expect respect from others in return for the respect we show them. Respect is an act of giving particular attention to a person (*Merriam-Webster's* 2016, 1143); it is a positive feeling of esteem or admiration for another person or entity.

Respect allows individuals to conduct themselves according to their culture's expectations. While spouses may constantly attempt to meet the expectations of their significant other, they are still likely to have arguments and disagreements from time to time. However, disrespectful behavior will not contribute to a successful marriage. For example, saying, "I don't feel you value what I have to offer or what I contribute to the relationship. You fail to recognize and respect my strengths and qualities," is a respectful way to voice concerns (May 2007, 31). Yelling, nagging, and belittling will not resolve anything because such actions are disrespectful and ineffective. The best way for couples to handle marital discord is through mutual respect, which ultimately leads to a successful marriage.

Respect must be shared between partners. The apostle Paul urged the wife to respect her husband in exchange for his love (Ephesians 5:33). "A husband is commanded to obey God by loving his wife, even if his wife does not obey the command of respect, and the wife is to obey the command to respect, even if the husband does not obey the commend to love" (Eggerichs 2004, 15).

A man generally struggles to demonstrate his love toward his wife unless she respects him accordingly. Paul told the Ephesians, "Each one of you also must love your wife as you love yourself and the wife must respect her husband" (Ephesians 5:33). Wives should accept their husbands as they are, not try to change them. Husbands have much to offer if they receive the space they need to be themselves. If a wife respects her husband, she can help him grow in the direction that he has chosen. When a wife honors her husband, she is honoring God; and when a wife dishonors her husband, she is dishonoring God (Pearl 2010, 22).

Married couples must communicate their needs, explain exactly what their priorities are, and subsequently respect each other's priorities. Instead of complaining about each other, partners should praise each other for the good things they have done. While complaining heightens tension, praise and prayer transform relationships. "Husband and wife who commit themselves to meet each other's most important needs will lay a foundation for lifelong happiness in a marriage relationship that is deeper and more satisfying than they ever dreamed possible" (Willard, 34).

Once a wife understands her husband's needs, the first thing she should try to do is to fulfill her obligations as a wife. A good wife is honest, sincere, and respectful of her husband's needs. Proverbs 31:10–15 (NIV) paints a picture of the ideal wife:

A wife of noble character who can find? She is worth far more than rubies. Her husband has full confidence in her and lacks nothing of value. She brings him good, not harm, all the days of her life. She selects wool and flax and works with eager hands. She is like the merchant ships, bringing her food from afar. She gets up while it is still dark; she provides food for her family and portions for her servant girls.

First Peter provides a clear example of how women can demonstrate respect to their husbands: "In the same way, you wives, be submissive to your own husbands so that even if any of them are disobedient to the word, they may be won without a word, by the behavior of their wives, as they observe you are morally pure in thought and respectful behavior" (1 Peter 3:1–2).

Certainly, a good husband will love his wife. If a husband loves his wife, he will also show respect for her. It can therefore be stated that love and respect walk together. No one wants to marry someone who would make a poor spouse because of a failure to learn how to show love and respect.

Husband and wife become one; therefore, the husband is not superior to the wife. Nonetheless, the wife is to respect her husband. "Respect is defined as to notice, regard, honor, prefer, defer to, encourage, love, and admire" (Driscoll and Driscoll 2012, 66). If a wife disrespects her husband, the husband may feel empty and start to think about ways to fill the emptiness.

The Bible established the institution of marriage to "complete" each partner is a loving, respectful relationship. God gave each party within a marriage its own responsibility. The man's responsibility is to love his wife as he loves himself. It is not easy to find someone who hates himself. If a man therefore loves himself, he must also love his wife in the same way. The responsibility of the wife is to respect her husband. Because no woman likes to disrespect herself, she will respect her husband in the same way that she respects herself. This is how God intended for married men and women to live in order to have a successful marriage. We have to live the married life according to the way God planned it.

When the wife says "I do," that means she is under the authority of her husband and owes him respect and submission. No woman can say that she respects God if she does not respect her husband. The word *hupokouo* is from the Greek words *hupo*, which means "under," and *akouo*, which means "I hear." When these two words are combined, they picture someone who is *hupo*—under someone else's authority, and *akouo*—listening to hear that superior speaking to him (Renner 2003, 978). The word *hupokouo* implies that a submitting wife comes under the authority of her husband and listens to what he is saying.

On the other hand, a husband must protect his wife. How does he do this? A husband can protect his wife by praying for her. A protecting husband is a husband who loves his wife dearly. Remember Proverbs 18:22 (KJV), which says, "Whoso findeth a wife findeth a good thing, and obtaineth favour of the Lord." A husband should not allow the enemy to attack his wife in any way. A husband should not allow miscommunication to rule over the relationship between him and his wife. A good husband should not even allow the mistakes of the past to control the future of his marriage." When a wife knows that her husband is praying for her, it makes her feel loved and protected" (Omartian 2009, 27).

According to Stormie Omartian (2009, 25), "There are certain blessings God has for you just because you are married." Because God has declared that the two shall become one flesh, when one of the spouses is affected, the other one will also be affected. If the husband is happy, the wife will also be happy. If the husband is blessed, the wife will also be blessed. Certainly, that goes both ways. If the wife does not respect her husband and the husband does not love his wife, both of them will be unhappy. Her problems are his problems, just as his problems are her problems. This is the reason God said the two of them shall become one flesh: "Wherefore they are no more twain, but one flesh. What therefore God hath joined together, let no man put asunder" (Matthew 19:6 KJV). Without both husband and wife obeying God's commands, however, the marriage will not be successful. According to Michael Pearl (2012, 9), "Marriage is God's laboratory for perfecting the human race."

Let's take a brief side trip here and look at Adam's situation after creation. Adam was the first man created on the earth, and his job was to name all the animals. As he was doing his job, he discovered his need for a mate. He realized that he was lonely, and without a mate, life would not make any sense to him. Perhaps he came to this conclusion as he observed the animals he was naming. He likely noticed them relating to one another in pairs and groups. As he was working, he probably was thinking that something was wrong with him because, unlike the animals, he had no mate as his counterpart (Genesis 2:20). From the beginning, man recognized his deep need for a partner to walk through life with.

According to Dr. Eggerichs (2004, 16), wives have one driving need: they need to love and feel loved. They cannot be happy unless this need is met. Likewise, on the husband's side, his driving need is to feel respected. If that need is met, he will be happy and function better. Therefore, those who wish to have a successful marriage, enjoy peace in their homes, live with pure hearts, feel valued and close to each other, and experience marriage the way that God intended must apply the principles of love and respect. Love and respect are commanded by God Almighty; they are not optional and are not to be taken lightly. Without love and respect, no one will attain a successful marriage.

In reality, respect goes beyond husband and wife and affects the entire home. It is catastrophic when the husband does not respect God, the wife does not respect her husband, the husband does not love his wife, and children do not respect their parents. However, when respect and love are established according to God's will, everyone in the home reaps the benefits.

When the apostle Peter used the phrase "weaker vessel" in 1 Peter 3:7, he was referring to the wife. His implication is that every man is to treat his wife with care and gentleness. When something must be handled with care, it does not mean that the item is less expensive or of less value; in fact, the things that require special care sometimes have greater value than the things that do not require particular attention. Husbands should always view their wives as valuable and cherished. As

Proverbs 18:2 (KJV) reminds us, "Whoso findeth a wife findeth a good thing and obtaineth favour of the Lord."

Love and Respect in Everyday Life

Some families experience problems if the wives make more money than their husbands. Some women who earn more than their husbands disrespect them and try to make them feel inferior. Sometimes they even refuse to listen to their husbands. A wife, however, should never mock the ideas of her husband, because he is the protector. She should never put down him, his job, or his salary, in word or even in body language, because this kind of attitude is disrespectful.

Loving, supportive wives know how to make their husbands feel listened to and respected. These men are grateful to know that they are in good hands with a wife who is a true helpmate. Such women are always ready to light the candles when their husbands cannot afford to pay the light bill. Instead of putting their husbands down, these wives share good ideas and try to be a part of the solution. They quickly and respectfully voice their concerns about finances and then offer suggestions on how to cut spending until the situation improves. In conclusion, "The key to creating fond feelings of love in a husband toward his wife is through showing him unconditional respect" (Eggerichs 2004, 19).

Accordingly, a man can foster respect from his wife by leading through example. "Therefore whatever you desire for men to do to you, you shall also do to them; for this is the law and the prophets" (Matthew 7:12 NIV). What Matthew is telling married men in this verse is for them to be proactive in their marriage. Instead of waiting for their wives to treat them with respect and dignity, they should start showing her the love they would like to receive for themselves. One thing we all know is that everybody likes to receive love.

The Bible's instruction in this matter is clear. Second Corinthians 9:7 (NIV) says, "Each one must give as he has decided in his heart, not reluctantly or under compulsion, for God loves a cheerful giver"; and Luke 6:31 (NIV) says, "As you would like people to do to you, do exactly so to them" (Luke 6:31 NIV). First Peter 3:7 (NIV) carries the meaning into the marriage relationship, saying, "Married men, in the same way, live with your wives with a clear recognition of the fact that they are weaker than you. Yet, since you are heirs with them of God's free gift of life, treat them with honor; so that your prayers may not be hindered."

Chapter 7: Love

There are three types of love: *agape*, *eros*, and *philos*. In this chapter, we are going to take a look at them, one by one. First is *agape* love.

Agape is God's kind of love. It is unconditional; there is nothing we must do to be loved by God. "For God so loved the world that he gave his only begotten Son, that whosoever believeth in him should not perish, but have everlasting life" (John 3:16 KJV). According to Renner (2003, 671), "*Agape* is a divine love that gives and gives, even when it is not responded to, thanked, or acknowledged." *Agape* love is not based on response, but on a decision to keep on loving, regardless of a recipient's response or lack of response. Because it is unconditional, it is the highest, noblest, purest form of love that exists (671). It is a concept comparable to *true love*, a term frequently used to describe the love between a husband and a wife and their family. In order for a marriage to succeed, a tremendous amount of unconditional love is required.

In Psalm 57, the psalmist said, "Thy mercy, O Lord, is in the heavens; and thy faithfulness reacheth unto the clouds" (Psalm 57:11 KJV). In the New Testament, the apostle Paul declared the unconditional love of God when he wrote, "Who shall separate us from the love of Christ?" (Romans 8:35 KJV). God's love is unconditional, incomparable, and above all things. The best relationships between husbands and wives are built on this agape foundation of love and trust.

Again, agape love is an unconditional love. It describes the love that should exist between family members and people in highly committed relationships. An example of agape love is the love of a parent for his or her child. In many parent-child relationships, no matter what happens—including arguments, differences in belief, or opposite political affiliations—the bond remains unchanging and unconditional. Generally speaking, there are no conditions or limitations that govern a mother's ability to continue loving her child. Her child does not have to maintain a certain standard in order to ensure her maternal love. Jesus's love for humanity is an even better example of agape love. Even after all Jesus was subjected to, His words on the cross were "Father, forgive them; for they know not what they do" (Luke 23:34 NIV). His love for humanity was, and is, unconditional.

In 1 Corinthians 13:4 (NIV), Paul wrote, "Love is patient; love is kind. It does not envy, it does not boast; it is not proud." In this verse, the apostle Paul shares the five primary characteristics of agape love. In order to achieve a successful marriage, it is important to manifest all of these characteristics. According to Rick Renner (2003, 671), agape love is unlike any other love in the world. It is a divine love that continuously gives even when it receives negative responses or no acknowledgment at all. The apostle Paul used the word *agape* to describe the highest level of love; this is also the kind of love that God expects for every married man and woman to share with each other. This kind of love is completely different from the love the world offers.

What are the characteristics of agape love, in addition to the ones mentioned above? The apostle Paul uses the words *charity* and *long-suffering* to describe God's love (Renner 2003, 671). Gertzen (2014) sheds light on this from a slightly different angle:

For Peter, sharing in ministry means sharing in suffering: suffering now and glory to come. . . . If all Christians partake of Christ's suffering and glory, how much more must the shepherds of his flock do so (1 Peter 5:1, New International Version). In the book of John, Jesus has a great conversation with Peter in regards of His lambs. "When they had finished eating, Jesus said to Simon Peter, 'Simon son of John, do you love me more than these?' 'Yes, Lord,' he said, 'You know that I love you.' Jesus said, 'Feed my lambs'" (John 21:15, New International Version). This exhortation to the leaders of the church to embrace suffering is clear in Peter's final charge to his "fellow elders" where he declares that he is not only a witness to Christ's sufferings, but also a participant or sharer in those sufferings.

Love means to commit yourself without guarantee, to give yourself completely in the hope that the love given will produce love in the recipient (Wright 2012, 153). According to Wright, "The perfect love would be one that gives all and expects nothing" (153). Agape love must be at the heart of a marriage in order for it to be successful. It is a self-giving love that keeps on going even when the other individual is unloving. As the apostle Paul instructed the Philippians, "Look not every man on his own things, but every man also on the things of others" (Philippians 2:4).

"Love doesn't demand others to be like itself; rather, it is so focused on the needs of others that it bends over backwards to become what others need it to be" (Renner 2003, 672). Likewise, do not expect that all actions of love will be manifested in the same specific way. According to Chapman and Bell (2011, 49), "Love is a verb. It may be found in serving others, or love may be expressed in words of encouragement. Love is not just a feeling. It's a choice. It's an action. Love is a verb."

According to Chapman (2010, 108), there are five love languages: (1) words of affirmation, (2) acts of service, (3) receiving gifts, (4) quality time, and (5) physical touch. These languages help people better understand the ways in which they and the important people in their lives perceive and experience love. For example, if a wife's love language is acts of service, her husband can manifest his love by doing things that demonstrate a practical expression of love, such as maintaining her car in good working order, mowing the lawn, and staying on top of household repairs. Similarly, if a husband's love language is words of affirmation, his wife can express her love by speaking words of encouragement to him.

Couples who understand and display agape love do not throw away their wedding rings and quit when the going gets rough. If a married couple sees that their patience with each other is about to run out, it's time for them to review their marriage vows and look inside their hearts for agape love. In the same vein, the apostle Paul teaches that "love is kind." According to Rick Renner (2003, 672), the word *kind* comes from the Greek word *chresteuoma*, which means to be able to adapt or comply with the needs of others. It means being always willing to serve and to change in order to meet the needs of others. "Kindness is love's willingness to enhance the life of another" (Wright 2012, 152).

Agape love is kind and given in spite of how the other person behaves. Agape love is a real love that resides inside the individual. When a husband goes above and beyond—meaning that he goes out of his way to make his wife feel loved—the wife most likely will respond by thanking him and showing love in return. How much more should we give thanks to our Lord for the constant ways He shows His unconditional love for His children. As Psalm 136:2 says, "His love endures."

Spouses who possess and display agape love are willing to serve. They are husbands and wives who are not preoccupied with self and self-interests; rather, they are ready to ask a very critical question: "Is there anything I can do for you?" Furthermore, this service is undergirded with an attitude and spirit of kindness. It is human nature to get annoyed or upset in the face of unpleasantries or when things do not go our way. However, agape love challenges spouses to maintain an attitude of kindness in performing acts of service and all the duties required in a marriage. With increased kindness, marital issues often decrease.

In 1 Corinthians 13, Paul continues to describe agape love and discusses the negative impact of envy. Envy, in the context in which Paul was speaking to the church at Corinth, is from the Greek word *zelos* and is used to describe those who are extremely consumed with their own aspirations or plans—individuals who will do anything in order to get their own way, even at the expense of others (Renner 2003, 672). A person like this is self-centered. On the other hand, God teaches that gentleness and kindness come through the sensitive and loving actions of His obedient servants (673).

Love is not just a feeling. It is a choice. It is an action that should be displayed on a daily basis. According to Chapman (2010, 49), "Love is a verb, which always conjugates itself with a subject to express something affirmative; with regard to loving a spouse, it is easy to give without loving, but it's almost impossible to love without giving." For example, a woman might express her appreciation for her husband through loving words. Likewise, sweet notes from a husband can make a wife feel good. Paul said to the Thessalonians, "We love you so much that we share with you not only God's good news but our own lives" (1 Thessalonians 2:8 NIV).

The Bible says only three things will abide until the end of time: "And now these three remain: faith, hope and love. But the greatest of these is love" (1 Corinthians 13:13). Love is the best thing a husband and wife can share. In order to have a successful marriage, love must be present, twenty-four hours a day, seven days a week, and 365 days a year.

Eros Love

The second type of love is *eros* love. "Uniquely, in classical love literature, the Greek novels as a genre portray eros as an amatory passion or a mutual bond between equals eventuating in marriage" (Konstan 2013, 49). Eros is primarily the physical and sensual love between a husband and a wife; however, eros also describes all emotional love and the overall feeling of love. Eros love is characterized by an insatiable desire to be near the one you love (Alston 1991, 385–395). It is entirely based on circumstances, and it is the target of emotion; therefore, it can change suddenly. As an emotion, it is morally neutral; however, it can easily lead to lust or passion. Eros can also be seen as the fruit of a new relationship. The word *eros* does not appear in the New Testament, but it is portrayed in the Old Testament in the Song of Songs (385–95).

Eros love should exist only in marriage because sex outside of marriage is sinful. For example, God did not approve of Solomon's thousands of women. In fact, He had warned him that they would encourage him to abandon the ways of his father, King David, who served the Lord Almighty (1 Kings 11:3 NIV). Obviously, God allowed Solomon to have these wives, but allowance is not the same as approval. Solomon's marital decisions were in direct violation of God's law, and there were consequences to his choices (1 Kings 11:3 NIV).

Like agape love, eros love an important form of love in a marriage and must be applied consistently. It is important because God commanded husbands and wives to engage in intimate sexual relations (Genesis 1:28). Sex itself is not a sin because without sex there would be no life. "Take ye wives, and beget sons and daughters; and take wives for your sons, and give your daughters to husbands, that they may bear sons and daughters; that ye may be increased there, and not diminished" (Jeremiah 29:6 KJV). However, sex outside of marriage is a sin in God's eyes, and it must be avoided in order for one's marriage to succeed.

A primary concern in marriage is whether or not a couple is spending enough time adoring each other the way God wants them to. The answer to that question will largely determine the quality not only of the marriage, but also of each partner's life.

Philos Love

The third kind of love is *philos* love. This kind of love is based on the friendship between two people (Renner 2003, 213); it is also referred to as platonic love. Furthermore, philos love is the kind of love that exists among brothers and sisters in Jesus Christ. Love for one's pastor, fellow church members, and congregation falls under the category of philos love. The difference between philos love and agape love is philos love is based on who a person is, but agape love is based on who God is. God's agape love, unlike philos love, does not depend on our love, but is unconditional.

According to Wright (2012, 161–162), "Some people equate being a pleaser with love. There are men and women in relationships, who constantly give and give, but it is not because of love. It is either because of guilt or because some of their needs are being met. Accordingly, "a pleaser is a person, who is dominated and guided by their own emotion." In addition, a pleaser is a person who does the right things but for the wrong reasons. A pleaser focuses on loving objects instead of being a loving person. This type of action is based not on agape love, but philos love.

How to Love

According to Chapman (2010, 18), God gives all of His people spiritual gifts and talents. These gifts are unique, and each one of us needs to learn to use our gifts accordingly. Through our individual gifts and abilities, God empowers us to love and serve other people. According to Kendall and Jones (2005, 25), "A Christian expects help from the Lord, just as a woman expects protection from her husband, and children expect protection from their parents." According to Wright (2012), marriage is an unconditional commitment to serve each other with love, as the Bible commands: "This is my commandment, That ye love one another, as I have loved you" (John 15:12 KJV).

In Psalm 128 (NIV), King David explains how a man who fears the Lord should behave and live. The psalmist starts with a beatitude: "Blessed are all who fear the LORD, who walk in obedience to him" (verse 1). The psalmist continues and compares a blessed man's wife to a fruitful vine. When a man loves his wife, he will cause her to thrive like a fruitful vine within his house (verse 3). Additionally, his children will be like olive shoots around the table (verse 3). Those are wonderful incentives reminding husbands to love their wives.

Love—or a lack thereof—is evident in the behavior spouses exhibit toward each other. In 1 Corinthians 13:4–8 (NIV), Paul not only explains what love does, but also what it does not do: "It does not envy, it does not boast, it is not proud. It does not dishonor others, it is not self-seeking, it is not easily angered, it keeps no record of wrongs. Love does not delight in evil but rejoices with the truth. It always protects, always trusts, always hopes, and always perseveres. Love never fails. But where there are prophecies, they will cease; where there are tongues, they will be stilled; where there is knowledge, it will pass away " (1 Cor 13:4-6 NIV}.

Jesus Himself said that the greatest act of love is to lay down one's life for another (John 15:13). This can be expanded to include spousal behavior, without necessarily meaning physical death. A man is to lay down his life for his wife through self-sacrifice, service, and long-suffering, and a wife is to do the same for her husband.

One way in which spouses demonstrate the behavior of laying down their lives is through prayer. Jesus modeled this in John 17 (KJV), when He told His Father, "I pray for them: I pray not for the world, but for them which thou hast given me; for they are thine" (verse 9). Certainly, a loving couple should always pray for each other, just as Jesus prayed for His church. Praying for someone shows that you care for that person, and prayer can open the door to greater levels of love and foster other marital benefits. When a wife knows that her husband is praying for her, it makes her feel loved, needed, and protected (Omartian 2009, 27). It makes her feel that she is important to him and that he cares for her. Prayer can soften a spouse's hardened heart, make things right between couples, enrich a couple's life together, and make their marriage run more smoothly. A spouse should always ask, "How do you want me to pray for you today?" (Omartian 2009, 27).

Just as women are created to nurture, men are created to protect and to fulfill the needs of women. There is a need met in a husband when his wife looks to him for protection. According to Michael Pearl (2012, 12), "Women expect protection from their husbands in the case of their enemies." Just as a Christian expects help from the Lord, a woman expects protection from her husband, and children also expect protection from their parents. This is all a part of the divine order, in which God placed the husband as the head of the house (Ephesians 5:23 KJV).

The Bible explains this very clearly: the husband is the leader of his home, and he must provide and maintain healthy control of his family. Timothy teaches that an overseer and deacon (male church leaders) must manage their families well (1 Timothy 3). First Timothy 3:5 specifically says, "If anyone does not know how to manage his own family, how can he take care of God's church.

The leadership role God has given man is not only a privileged position, but also a blessing and a great responsibility that requires much sacrifice and service (Ephesians 5:23). The Bible instructs us to "leave and cleave": "Therefore, shall a man leave his father and his mother, and shall cleave unto his wife: and they shall be one flesh" (Genesis 2:24). In order for a man and a woman to leave and cleave, much sacrifice is required from each of them in their respective responsibilities. The man is the leader and head of the house, but the woman is the neck that turns the head.

The apostle put it clearly in Ephesians, where he spells out the responsibilities of each family member. To the children, he says, "Children, obey your parents in the Lord, for this is right. 'Honor your father and mother'—which is the first commandment with a promise—'so that it may go well with you and that you may enjoy long life on the earth'" (Ephesians 6:1–3 NIV). Furthermore, the apostle addresses the duties of a parent to a child: "Fathers, do not exasperate your children; instead, bring them up in the training and instruction of the Lord" (verse 4).

With love, all is possible. Love is a feeling that someone experiences when one has a feeling that one has never felt before (Wright 2012, 141).

A loving relationship is a choice partnership. Loving someone with imperfections is seen as possibility and, therefore, a thing of beauty; where discovery, struggle, and acceptance are the basis of continued growth and wonderment. A loving relationship is one in which individuals trust each other enough to become vulnerable and secure, knowing the other person won't take advantage. It neither exploits nor takes the other for granted. It involves much communication, much sharing, and much tenderness. (Wright 2012, 158)

Love in a marriage relationship begins with love for the Lord: "And thou shalt love the LORD thy God with all thine heart, and with all thy soul, and with all thy might" (Deuteronomy 6:5 KJV). Without love, first for God and then for each other, it is impossible for a couple to maintain a lasting marriage. According to Dr. Eggerichs (2004, 40), when a wife is complaining, criticizing, or crying, she is sending a message to her husband: "I want your love."

The Bible uses the word *closeness* to describe the first marriage in human history, (Genesis 2:24 KJV). This was established by God, the creator of the universe. As believers, we know and believe in the love that God has for us, and that is the same love we must strive to demonstrate in our marriages. God is love, and the one who abides in love abides in God, and God abides in him (1 John 4:16). "What therefore God hath joined together, let not man put asunder" (Mark 10:9 KJV).

According to Smalley and Smalley (2015, 1), "Love is as long as we both shall live." After the marriage ceremony, the love life of the couple will be carefully observed by those around them. John 13:35 (KJV) reminds us, "By this shall all men know that ye are my disciples, if ye have love one to another," meaning that our love for our spouse proves to the world that we are a disciple of Jesus. In other words, people are watching the way we live out our lives.

One of the most memorable accounts of the manifestation of love is found in the Gospel of John. Six days before Passover, Jesus arrived in the village of Bethany and went to the home of His friend Lazarus. Unfortunately, Mary and Martha were in mourning because of the death of their brother, Lazarus. Jesus, however, raised Lazarus from the dead, and a dinner was prepared in His honor.

In the midst of this setting, sister Mary brought forth an expensive perfume made from essence of nard, a fragrance from the root of a plant grown in northern India. It was not a common product that people would have an abundance of lying around the house. It was expensive and for special use. Mary, wanting to manifest her unconditional love for Jesus, opened the perfume bottle, releasing its rich fragrance. Then she anointed Jesus' feet with it and wiped them with her hair. John 12:3 (KJV) says, "The house was filled with the odour of the ointment," symbolizing Mary's extravagant love for the Savior. Judas Iscariot, not understanding Mary's intent, commented harshly, "Why was not this ointment sold for three hundred pence, and given to the poor?" (verse 5)

Accordingly, one can give without loving, but no one can love without giving. Love is not just a good feeling for someone. Rather, love is an act of the will. Love, by its essence, results in action. It could be giving, forgiving, or patience, but something great will always come out of love (Chapman 2010, 5).

There is a need for a definition of love that is biblical rather than secular. The secular concept of love focuses on feelings. It has been said that "love is the feeling that you feel when you feel a feeling like you've never felt before" (Chapman 2010, 5). In the Bible, love is not automatically a feeling; love is an attitude that manifests in an appropriate behavior. It is the way in which we hold or carry our position. It is an attitude that chooses to build up another, to put someone else's interest above our own. Love is something someone chooses to do. This does not mean that the Bible makes no place for feelings; it does. The Bible does speak of romantic love, but understanding the broader biblical perspective on love will in turn enhance romantic love (Chapman, 2010, 5).

The apostle Paul says, "Look not every man on his own things, but every man also on things of others" (Philippians 2:4 KJV). In a loving relationship, each is concerned with the other, and each is prepared to do whatever it takes to protect the relationship and allow it to thrive. Love "suffers long," as it says in 1 Corinthians 13:4 (NKJV). This term is translated "patient" in other translations, meaning bearing pains or trials calmly or without complaint in love for others. Patience is one of the fruits of the Spirit (Galatians 5:22).

Those who possess patience are ready to endure as long as it takes to manifest their love for others. In this particular case, the "others" to be focused on are the wife and husband, as the Bible directs. The *fruit of the Holy Spirit* is a biblical term that references a person or community living in accord with the Holy Spirit and demonstrating His qualities. The fruit of the Spirit is an equalizer, which means a person who has the fruits of the Spirit at work will view everyone with the same eyes (Galatians 5:22). In addition, it is sacrificial: "Greater love has no man than this that a man lay down his life for his friends" (John 15:13 KJV).

Furthermore, "suffers long" describes a person who manifests love under provocation or strain. Love passionately and patiently bears with others as long as necessary. Love does not demand others to be like itself, but instead is focused on the needs of others (Sparking Gems 91, 673). Accordingly, whenever love is in the heart, it will flow out to others in love and blessings.

The love of Jesus is beyond comparison. Every act of His life demonstrated divine compassion. His heart went out in tender sympathy to the children of men. The poorest or least of men was not afraid to approach Him, and little children were attracted to Him. The story of Zacchaeus puts on display this unwavering love that Jesus had for those rejected by society. Luke 19:2–4 (KJV) says, "There was a man named

Zacchaeus, which was the chief among the publicans [tax collectors], and he was rich. And he sought to see Jesus who he was; and could not for the press, because he was little of stature. And he ran before, and climbed up into a sycamore tree to see him: for he was to pass that way." (Luc 19:2-4 KJV).

Despite this fact, however, Jesus still visited his house. Jesus' love for this social outcast was stronger than anything anyone could say against Zacchaeus. Suddenly Jesus called for Zacchaeus to come down from the sycamore tree, because He wanted to go to his house. Zacchaeus was a tax collector and thus hated by his own people. This was of no concern to Jesus, and He ignored the criticism of the judgmental bystanders. Zacchaeus, well aware of his condition, confessed to Jesus that he was a lost sinner and made clear his intent to change: "And Zacchaeus stood, and said unto the Lord: Behold, Lord, the half of my goods I give to the poor" (Luke 19:8 KJV). Unlike the rich, young ruler, he immediately volunteered his wealth. "And if I have taken anything from any man by false accusation, I restore him fourfold," he added.

Jesus never suppressed one word of truth, but He exercised the greatest of tact and thoughtful attention in His discourse with people. Jesus was never rude, never needlessly spoke a severe word, and never gave needless pain to a sensitive soul. Jesus did not censure human weakness, but He spoke the truth in love. He said in John 8:32 (NIV), "Then you will know the truth, and the truth will set you free." Jesus denounced hypocrisy, unbelief, and iniquity. He wept over Jerusalem, the city that He loved: "When he drew near and saw the city, he wept over it" (John 19:41). They refused to receive Him—the way, the truth, and the life. They rejected Him, the Savior, but He regarded them with tender pity. Jesus's life was one of self-denial and thoughtful care for others. Every soul was precious in His eyes. Though He ever bore Himself with divine dignity, He bowed with tender regard to every member of the family of God. In all men He saw fallen souls whom it was His mission to love and save.

Chapter 8: Building a Family

———∞———

The concept of family was part of God's original plan, and it is one of His greatest gifts to humankind. God, the creator of the universe, told Adam and Eve in the Garden of Eden, "Be fruitful, and multiply, and replenish the earth, and subdue it" (Genesis 1:28). Having babies is a natural part of creation. When men and women decide to have children, they reproduce what God started in the Garden of Eden.

A family begins with a married couple, but it grows when the wife gives birth. Children play a large role in a couple's life after marriage. Because babies bring joy to their families, they cement a union as a physical manifestation of their parents' love. Children bring happiness to their parents and should be considered a blessing. If partners are unable to have children, they often experience a great deal of pain.

For example, in 1 Samuel, Hannah suffered terribly when she was unable to become pregnant (1 Samuel 1:7–10). Day and night, she cried to the Lord from the temple. Her expression of pain was so great that many people, including Eli, the priest of the temple, thought that Hannah was drunk (1 Samuel 1:13). Hannah did not leave the temple until God heard her prayers and blessed her with a son, whom she named Samuel (1 Samuel 2:1–10). When her son was born, Hannah's sorrow was washed away. She sang to the Lord, and joy returned to her heart. Hannah was thankful to the Lord, and she gave her son back to Him.

From Scripture, it is obvious that God loves babies. When the baby Jesus was born, God the Father sent all the stars and the three wise men to Bethlehem to worship Him (Matthew 2:2). According to the Gospel of Matthew, Jesus loves little children. Many times people brought their children to Jesus to be blessed. On one occasion, the disciples rebuked the parents for bringing their children, but Jesus said, "Suffer little children, and forbid them not, to come unto me: for of such is the kingdom of heaven" (Matthew 19:14 KJV).

According to Dr. James Dobson (2004, 13), "The traditional family and marriage has been defined from the beginning of time and are among the few institutions that have, in fact, stood the test of time." Family is more important than anything else, so having a baby is often the next step after getting married. During biblical times—perhaps even more so than today—couples who were unable to have children often suffered terribly. Take, for example, the story of Abraham and Sarah.

Abraham was a great man of God. Abraham, at one hundred years of age, and his wife, Sarah, at ninety, did not have any children (Genesis 17:17). At this advanced age, they were hopeless in regard to having a baby. But God told Abraham, "Fear not, Abram: I am thy shield and thy exceeding great reward" (Genesis 15:1 KJV). Desperately, Abram said, "Lord God, what wilt thou give me, seeing I go childless, and the steward of my house is this Eliezer of Damascus?" (Genesis 15:2). Abraham's pain and fear of Sarah's barrenness was evident in his response. Fortunately, when the angel of the Lord visited Abraham and Sarah's house and told Abraham that he would be the father of a multitude, the couple reclaimed their joy.

Originally, sin became part of humanity after the fall in the Garden of Eden. Therefore, human beings have a proclivity to make choices that disobey God's will. In that vein, instead of creating a family structured after God's design, some individuals desire to change their nature to function as members of the opposite sex. Essentially, some men want to be women, and some women want to be men. However, God will not change His plan just because some individuals are not satisfied with the gender they were born with (Romans 1:26–32). God will not change His original plan in regard to marriage and reproduction.

Scripture is clear about deviating from God's plan for human sexuality: "For this cause God gave them up unto vile affections; for even their women did change the natural use into that which is against nature" (Romans 1:26). Same-sex marriage is not something to be taken lightly. It is a sin because same-sex couples cannot reproduce, and God's plan for men and women is that they multiply and fill the earth (Genesis 1:22). Originally, God created neither two men nor two women; he created one man and one woman. In addition, He created the entire universe with complementary males and females. Even before the flood, God told Noah to take a pair of each animal: "Of every clean beast you shall take to you by sevens, the male and his female" (Genesis 7:2). The divine intent is clear.

Starting a Family

What is a family, and what makes a complete family? "A family is a group consisting of parents and children living together in a household. Husband and wife unite as one; they build a new family together" (*Merriam-Webster's* 2016). In some cultures, family members also include grandparents, aunts, and uncles. In any case, families are constantly growing and changing.

In order for a man to begin his own family, he must first find a woman who completes him. This woman has a very specific, important responsibility: "By placing the specific, personal experiences of individual women in a larger social and economic framework, the women's work at home is one of the most important and necessary labour processes of industrial capitalist society" (Luxton 1980, 13).

Just as it is now, the family was the most important unit of society in Bible days:

The family was the central unit of Hebrew society, and the concept of the family was often extended to refer to tribes, to the kingdoms of Israel and Judah, and to the Israelites as a whole. Man's relation to God and his fellow-covenanters are also described in the language of family relations, in such terms as father, son, children, and brethren, the "household of God," and "household of faith." (Layman 1964, 245)

Family matters should be a priority in any marriage, so couples should begin thinking about family well-being even before marriage. There are many reasons for a couple to eventually start a family. Individuals usually love to have people in their lives to whom they can give love and expect to receive love. The loving relationship between family members has no comparison.

"For a family to experience joy there needs to be a firm foundation" (Stone, 36). Children need to see their parents interacting and enjoying each other's conversation and company. They need a model of faithfulness and healthy negotiation. Accordingly, family members should maintain daily routines, including work, play, housework, and projects, that bring personal satisfaction to one another. They should be convinced that these routines are God's will and purpose to glorify Him (Minirth, 144). Minirth goes on to say, "Set aside time daily for intimacy with God, including prayer and Scripture meditation. Set aside enough time to continually build a more and more intimate relationship with your mate. This includes time for fun, fellowship, serious communication, have a good sex life. Your mate should be an even higher priority than your children" (144).

Having Children

Children are an integral part of the family unit. Although some people choose not to have children or are unable to do so, the family dynamic often lacks something if children are absent. Luke 1:5–25 records the story of a man named Zacharias and his wife, Elisabeth. They were blameless and great servants of the Lord, but Elisabeth was barren. The Bible says that they were old and righteous but lacked joy because of their childlessness. While Zacharias was burning incense in the temple one day, something extraordinary happened: "There appeared unto him an angel of the Lord standing on the right side of the altar of incense" (Luke 1:11 KJV). The angel had a message from God: "Fear not, Zacharias: for thy prayer is heard; and thy wife Elisabeth shall bear thee a son, and thou shalt call his name John. And thou shalt have joy and gladness; and many shall rejoice at his birth" (Luke 1:13–14 KJV). The word of the Lord proved true, and John the Baptist came into the world to prepare the way for Jesus, the Messiah.

Having children is important, but raising them is even more important. It requires hard work, and the responsibility should not be taken lightly. A biblical foundation is the best guide on how parents should raise their children. For example, the Bible tells parents to "teach [God's laws] diligently unto thy children, and . . . talk of them when thou sittest in thine house, and when thou walkest by the way, and when thou liest down, and thou risest up" (Deuteronomy 6:7 KJV). Both parents should be active in raising the children according to God's Word, sharing responsibility and accountability.

Ultimately, a married couple decides how many children they can afford in terms of financial, physical, emotional, and other resources. Regardless of the number, the key to raising children is to establish a solid system at home in which the children can grow up secure and fulfilled.

Facebook Pinterest

In order to have successful families, couples must strive to have the right mind-set even before becoming parents. To become good parents, they must accept the same responsibilities that God assigned to Adam and Eve when He told them to "be fruitful, and multiply, and replenish the earth, and subdue it" (Genesis 1:28 NIV). In reproducing, couples adhere to the Word of God, and in doing so, they will experience much joy within the family.

Though both parents share responsibility in raising their children, their roles are different. Let's look first at the role of the mother. In the Bible, mothers are admonished to love their children. As the apostle Paul explained in the book of Titus, the responsibility of older women is to "teach the young women to be sober, to love their husbands, to love their children, to be discreet, chaste, keepers at home, good, obedient to their own husbands, that the word of God be not blasphemed" (Titus 2:4–5 KJV). Very often, a young mother has no knowledge of how to raise her children in the right way. For example, she may be too permissive, not understanding that she needs to reprimand her children when they make a mistake. Otherwise, it will be easy for them to become spoiled. When a mother loves her children very much, it is a great thing; but if that love is excessive, it will only cause damage to the child's future (Bhikkhu 2015, 1). This is where an older, more experienced mother comes in; she may be able to gently guide the young mother on a more solid, biblical path. The key to raising a well-rounded child is to establish a solid support system at home so that she grows up satisfied with her achievements and ambitions. "The goal as a parent is to help your child feel competent and confident, and to help her develop a sense of passion and purpose" (Author, year, page number).

The apostle Paul wrote, "The Christian woman will be saved in childbearing if she continues in faith, love, and holiness, with self-control" (1 Timothy 2:15 KJV). Paul is not saying a woman's salvation is contingent on being able to reproduce; rather, he is addressing the basic design, function, and need of a woman. The Word of God does not condemn a married mother for working; however, it does teach that the woman is to put her family and home first. Sadly, many women today want to focus on their careers to the exclusion of getting married and starting a family. Being a mother comes with its own rewards, however. One of the greatest compliments to a wife and mother is found in Proverbs 31:28, which reads, "Her children rise up and call her blessed; her husband also, and he praises her."

In the same way that women have an important role to play in the lives of their children, so, too, do men, the fathers, have an important place within the family unit. A father serves as a guide for his children. Children often become delinquent when their fathers leave them alone to make their own decisions. The first lessons a child learns are not in the classroom, but in the home. The best place for a boy to learn how to be a man is in the home, where he can observe his own father.

Many men do not spend enough time with their children. The pressures of making a living create all sorts of problems. Nevertheless, the most important responsibility of a father is to provide a future for his children. His words should teach his children how to live upright lives. Children do not know if their actions are right or wrong; therefore, it is up to the father and the mother to correct them before it is too late (Bhikkhu 2015, 5).

Psalm 128:3 (NIV) describes what a good father looks like: "Your wife shall be as a fruitful vine by the sides of your house: your children like olive plants around your table." When a father creates a safe and loving environment for his offspring, he instills in them a sense of hope. Hope is an optimistic attitude of mind based on an expectation of positive outcomes related to events and circumstances in one's life or the world at large. As a verb, its definitions include "expect with confidence" and "to cherish." A man who instills hope in his family fulfills what 3 John 1:2 (KJV) says: "Beloved, I wish above all things that thou mayest prosper and be in health, even as thy soul prospereth."

A young man and a young woman who decide to get married should realize that they are, in essence, "little gods" who will create life. Most husbands and wives would love to have children, regardless of their economic situation (Bhikkhu, 2015, 4). Ephesians 6 outlines the biblical hierarchy for a family.

Through Thick and Thin

Hope, as mentioned above, is also important for parents. In fact, all human beings need hope; without it, life comes to a standstill. According to Wright and Roberts (1997, 7), "The marriage relationship is a school, a learning and growing environment in which if everything is as it should be, both partners can grow and develop." Unfortunately, to many people, divorce is viewed as an easy solution when problems arise after marriage, especially when both individuals believe that marital life should be simple and free from complications. However, problems will occur, and when they do, they need to be fixed. Cultivating self-discipline and carefully setting a good example are essential elements in a long-term marriage that stands the test of time.

This, of course, is not easy. Parents must train themselves to exercise self-discipline. It is not a good idea for them to do things in accordance with their natural desires. They should always provide an example for their children to emulate. If parents don't do what is right, their children will follow suit. On the other hand, their children will surely remember the good examples they are taught. The parents' example supersedes anything else their children will learn. When children do good, they must be complimented, and bad actions should be criticized. According to Bhikkhu (2015, 7), this is an important principle. When parents are raising children, they must teach them through consistent repetition, because this will ensure that their children become good citizens.

Divorce is not the solution for marital discord, but it is often seen as a way to escape difficulty and unwanted responsibilities. Researchers find that most children from divorced families function normally, but some clinicians assert that young people are disturbed even many years after their parents have been divorced.

To raise children who are mentally healthy, parents must feed their children the right foods for their minds. According to Bhikkhu (2015, 10), they must eat foods that will not poison their minds. Parents must try to prevent this from happening at every cost. If it does happen, parents must do everything in their power to treat the illness quickly and adequately.

In general, when someone consistently does good, good will follow. This happens because a repeated action will eventually become a habit. It's important to raise children with great habits that will serve them well in life. Developing a great habit might be very difficult at the beginning, but with enough repetition and commitment, it will become easy. In addition, it's also very important for a newly married couple to develop the habits that will allow them to build the right foundation for their lives together and for any children they will have.

According to Zig Ziglar (1985, 20), "Developing self-control often requires painful learning experiences, but the result is well worth the effort." Likewise, building a family requires self-control and unconditional love to develop healthy relationships. For instance, in any family there will always be discussion and conflict about responsibilities. The daily functioning of the home, however, provides excellent opportunities for teaching family values and responsibilities (Ziglar 1985, 48). The wife should not worry about the responsibilities of the husband, because he will do the best he can to take care of his responsibilities. Likewise, the man should not worry about the responsibilities of his wife, trusting that she will fulfill them. For example, while the husband is at work, the wife will drop the kids off at school and pick them up at the end of the day.

In order to build a successful family, a couple must first identify the obstacles to that success, the hindrances that stand between them and the success of the family. For starters, it might be helpful to ask, what is a family man? A family man is a "man who has a wife and children and who is devoted to his family and his home" (*Merriam-Webster's* 2016, 488). Family values involve all the ideas of how to live his family life, and these are often passed down from previous generations. A family man helps define appropriate and inappropriate behavior in various situations, trains his children to make good choices, and identifies the bond that his family shares. If a family doesn't already have these values in place, a family man will recognize the importance of applying these in order to achieve success.

Having a family is so important. For example, God used Noah's family to replenish the earth after the deluge of the flood. According to Genesis 6, Noah had a beautiful family, including his wife, three sons, and the wives of the three sons. "Noah and his entire family found grace in the eyes of the Lord" (Genesis 6:8 KJV), and God Almighty saved them. The deluge was one of a kind, destroying all but Noah, his family, and the animals on the ark. When they were finally able to disembark, "God blessed Noah and his sons, and said unto them, Be fruitful, and multiply, and replenish the earth" (Genesis 9:1 KJV).

Very often, people do not understand the meaning of marriage and family. They just meet someone and decide to get married without acquiring the knowledge and skills necessary to take care of each other. Without acquiring the necessary knowledge before entering into a marriage relationship, a man and woman will not be able to have a successful marriage. Before entering marriage, it's important to possess the skills and knowledge needed to meet the emotional, physical, and mental needs of one's partner.

According to Smalley and Smalley (2015, 184), in the society in which we live, a person is required to have four to five years of training before receiving an electrician's license, four years before a nursing license, and four years to become a chef in a good restaurant or a hotel, but absolutely no training for a marriage license. The Bible says—and this applies to marriage as well as spiritual learning—"My people are destroyed for lack of knowledge: because thou hast rejected knowledge, I will also reject thee" (Hosea 4:6 KJV). *Merriam-Webster's Dictionary* (2016, 748) defines knowledge as "as far as one knows; within the range of one's information." Philosophers have been studying knowledge for as long as philosophy has been around. It's one of those perennial topics, like the nature of matter in the hard sciences, that has been continually refined since before the time of Plato.

Nonetheless, knowledge is critical to marriage. It is not normal for a man to marry without knowing how to talk to his wife. In reality, however, many men do not even know that their wives need intimate communication. Very often, a man is completely unaware that his wife has a sensitive side to her nature. Likewise, many women step into marriage similarly handicapped. They do not understand that admiration is to a man what romance is to a woman. They do not understand that a man generally relies on reasoning rather than intuitive sensitivity (Smalley and Smalley 2015, 184). The bottom line is that no one should enter marriage without possessing the knowledge that will permit it not just to survive, but to thrive.

Unresolved Issues from the Past

Unresolved issues from the past are unhealthy for the future of a family and are one of the issues that partners must have knowledge of. According to Smalley and Smalley (2015), marriage is simply two imperfect people committing to live life together forever. A good marriage goes through the mysterious, holy metamorphosis of becoming one flesh, ironing out the problems that arise either from the past or the present. One of the reasons some people are afraid to create a family is that they believe marriage itself creates problems. Living life together as a couple with a mortgage and children is not simple, but running away from unresolved issues is not the solution.

When a wife believes in her husband and deeply respects him, he gains the confidence necessary to compete successfully and live responsibly. She gives him a reason to harness his masculine energy, to build a home, obtain and keep a job, help her raise their children, remain sober within the law, spend money wisely, etc. Without positive feminine influence, his tendency is to release the power of testosterone in a way that is destructive to himself and to society at large. (Dobson, 10)

Sadly, there will be conflict in any marriage because conflict is a fact of life. According to Wright (2012, 62), conflict is defined as a clash, struggle, or sharp disagreement over interests or ideas. "Why does conflict occur? The answer is simply that we are human beings, imperfect people whom God graciously loves in spite of our imperfection." From the Bible, we know our fallen state—"For all have sinned, and come short of the glory of God" (Romans 3:23 KJV); and "There is none righteous, no, not one" (Romans 3:10 KJV)—yet we know He accepts and loves us unconditionally.

We all hold unshakable opinions on important issues and generally believe we are right in the actions we take. Whenever opinions differ, however, conflict often occurs. Conflict is normal and even healthy as part of a relationship. Two people cannot be expected to agree on everything at all times. Conflicts are inevitable, so learning how to handle them in a healthy way is very important (Wright 2012, 62).

When a problem arises in a family, it needs to be solved, and forgiveness will have to apply and normal life must continue. Many people only change when crisis demands it. We go on a diet after our doctors say we are in danger, make a budget after we are in significant debt, and go to marriage counselors or pastors after the possibility of divorce has been put on the table. It is far wiser and more helpful to make changes before crisis demands it. (Driscoll and Driscoll 2012, 219).

Accordingly, one of the reasons so many people are unhappy and unsuccessful in their marriage is because they enter into it unprepared, full of wonderful, and often unrealistic, dreams about what their marriage will be like. They fail to take into account their differences with their spouse, differences established in the process of growing up. Most of us observed our parents, who served as role models, and we identify with them by responding to life in a similar fashion. Sometimes, however, we respond to life in the opposite way, reacting to what we felt was negative in our upbringing. Everyone develops a unique pattern of responding to life emotionally, socially, intellectually, and spiritually (Chapman 2010, 109).

Differences are also rooted in the fact that we are unique creatures of almighty God. God is infinitely creative, so every human being has his or her own fingerprints. No human being is exactly like another human being. Everyone is a God-made original: "For thou hast possessed my reins: thou hast covered me in my mother's womb. I will praise thee; for I am fearfully made: marvellous are thy works; and that my soul knoweth right well" (Psalm 139:13–14 KJV).

The Bible tells us that diversity does not necessitate division: "Even so the body is not made up of one part but of many" (1 Corinthians 12:14 NIV). Spouses must learn how to appreciate each other's differences, but this is almost impossible to do without understanding the concept of God-given uniqueness. It is easy to become frustrated when situations arise, and ask, "God, why is my spouse so different?" However, it is better to say, "Thank you, God, for that difference" (Wright 2012, 65).

Chapter 9: Those Who Oppose Marriage

Despite the benefits of marrying and having children, some people are opposed to the idea. In fact, some people prefer instead to have sexual partners, their rationale being that they will not have to face the prospect of divorce because they have no intention of being married in the first place. In addition, by not marrying, they do not have to assume full responsibility for a spouse, because they only have sexual partners. These sexual partners can be of either gender or any sexual orientation. The relationship may be either exclusive or casual.

Extramarital sex, however, violates God's will. Couples should not engage in sexual activities if they are unmarried. As Paul wrote, "Now concerning the things whereof ye wrote unto me: It is good for a man not to touch a woman. Nevertheless, to avoid fornication, let every man have his own wife, and let every woman have her own husband" (1 Corinthians 7:2). According to Paul, it is imperative that men and women who fear God avoid fornication. Paul warns, "Neither let us commit fornication, as some of them committed, and fell in one day three and twenty thousand" (1 Corinthians 10:8 NIV). Galatians 5:19 states, "Now the works of the flesh are manifest, which are these: adultery, fornication, uncleanness, and lasciviousness" (Galatians 5:19 NIV).

Sadly, many people today, including many "Christians," do not consider their bodies to be temples of the Holy Spirit; instead, they make their bodies into temples of lust (Colossians 3:5). *Lust* is defined as an emotion or feeling of intense desire in the body or a strong feeling of sexual desire (*Merriam-Webster's*, 2016, 455). In 2 Timothy, Paul advises Christian youth to flee from lust: "Flee also youthful lust; but follow righteousness, faith, charity, peace, with them that call on the Lord out of a pure heart" (2 Timothy 2:22 KJV).

Lust is a powerful psychological force producing intense longing for an object or circumstance to fulfill one's emotions. It appears with regulaitry in college, high school, and even junior high school curriculum. Consequently, sexuality textbooks now abound, and it is to one of these texts that a student interested in sexual desire is likely to go to learn more about the subject. (Regan and Berscheid 1999, 1)

Lust can take on many forms, such as the lust for knowledge, the lust for sex, or the lust for power. Lusting for something is distinct from needing it. Lust implies a degree of excess, that which is unnecessary. God wants everyone to realize his or her full potential, to be thankful, and to enjoy life to the fullest, but not to lust after anything. Gratitude is critical in whatever situation life brings and will help safeguard against lust.

Although marriage is a blessed institution, it brings no guarantee of ease. Individuals may marry someone, discover many things about their spouse, and subsequently wish they were single again. Certainly, there will be difficulties in marriage, and problems will arise from time to time. However, when a difficult situation arises, Christians must allow God to take control, for He knows what is best for His children.

There are blessings in both singleness and married life. A single person can devote all of his or her time to the Lord. (Hebrews 13:5 KJV). Both states are valid, and both yield spiritual blessings.

As stated in the previous chapter, 1 Corinthians 12:14 illustrates that diversity does not necessitate division: "Now the body is not made up of one part but of many." Certainly, a husband and a wife are two parts in one body, but they are each a unique individual. The word *unique* means "one of a kind," and the perfect example of this is Jesus, the unique Son of God (John 3:16). Couples must understand that uniqueness is something that God implants in everyone as a gift. One person's uniqueness should not be compared to another's.

At times, married people may ask God how their spouse is different or special compared to someone else. This sort of positive thinking is necessary and can help a marriage to become successful. On the other hand, some people are simply dream killers. One spouse should not tell the other spouse that his or her ambitions are wrong unless they are not in accordance with the Word of God. If spouses' beliefs differ, they should not jump to conclusions about each other. It is better to think twice before correcting or killing the other's dreams, always remembering that God made each of us different and unique.

Differences in a marriage are not uncommon. Yes, every person who marries has characteristics similar to the one he or she marries, but he or she also has many that are different. Different ways of perceiving, thinking, feeling, and behaving are part of marital adjustment. Differences are important because it holds out the promise of need fulfillment for each person. (Wright 2012, 13)

God's plan is for men and women to marry. Nowhere in the Bible do we see "sexual partners" listed as a viable alternative to marriage. Depending on the version, Genesis 2:18 uses the terms *partner*, *helper*, *helpmeet*, *helpmate*, and *companion*. Condoned sexual relationships in the Bible identify sexual partners as husband and wife; there is no such thing as a sexual partner outside of marriage. Oftentimes, however, we see individuals living together as man and wife even though they are not married. This is not right, according to the Bible. In the Old Testament, King David and his son King Solomon had many sexual partners; however, this was never God's intent. When individuals are living in fornication, they may enjoy spending time together, but their actions defy the Word of God. Genesis 2:24 (KJV) instructs that "a man [shall] leave his father and his mother, and shall cleave unto his wife: and they shall be one flesh." This concept must be understood: a man and a woman must be married in order to be sexual partners. Adultery is defined as having sexual intercourse with a person other than one's spouse (Exodus 20:14). The revelation to Christians, however, is that each man should have his own wife, and each wife her own husband (1 Corinthians 7:2).

This is true in the heart, as well in the Word of God. More than one wife and more than one husband is forbidden, and sexual intercourse with anyone beside one's wife or one's husband is forbidden" (Exodus 20:14). You shall not covet your neighbor's house, or wife, or his male servant, or his female servant, or his ox, or his donkey, or anything that is your neighbor's" (Exodus 20:17 ESV). "Likewise, you shall not commit adultery" (Exodus 20:14 ESV). This is God's command. There is no way around it.

Two reasons individuals may engage in extramarital affairs are an overload of responsibilities and marital difficulties. However, this does not have to mean the end of the marriage. "For I know the plans I have for you, declares the Lord, plans to prosper you and not to harm you, plans to give you hope and a future" (Jeremiah 29:11 NIV). Each person has been spiritually preprogrammed to live a victorious life. No one is created to be average, to drag around, or to barely make it, living defeated and depressed. "The Lord will make you the head, not the tail. If you pay attention to the commands of the Lord your God that I give you this day and carefully follow them, you will always be at the top, never at the bottom" (Deuteronomy 28:13 NIV).

In effect, people were created to be happy, healthy, and whole, both as individuals and in the context of marriage. Scripture says, "Let us make mankind in our image, in our likeness, so that they may rule over the fish in the sea and the birds in the sky, over the livestock and all the wild animals, and over all the creatures that move along the ground" (Genesis 1:26 NIV). God is our heavenly Father; we all possess some of His knowledge and some of His characteristics. With God on our side, there is truly nothing to fear. As Deuteronomy 3:16 (NIV) says, "Be strong and courageous. Do not be afraid or terrified for anything because the Lord your God goes with you." Equally, Scripture says in Psalm 37:25, "I have been young, and now am old; yet have I not seen the righteous forsaken, nor his seed begging bread." God takes care of His own; no one should be afraid of doing the right thing.

Sometimes people live together for many years, happy to be free from the responsibility that marriage would bring. In such a situation, either partner could leave the relationship at any time with minimal repercussions. However, years of unmarried cohabitation in order to avoid responsibility is an attempted shortcut to success, and it could be catastrophic.

For some men and women, however, shortcuts are part of their lives. They are always looking for the best way to save time, money, and avoid responsibility. When talking about human relationships, it is unfair to live with someone for years and then decide to move out because you want to pursue a new relationship. This can only happen, though, when a couple decides not to marry, and it is contrary to Scripture: "Do to others as you would have them do to you" (Luke 6:31 NIV).

It seems that fewer and fewer people are getting married these days, and even fewer men than women seem interested in the construct. Individuals no longer embrace marriage as their families did in the past. Regardless, the Bible argues, that "two are better than one, because they have a good return for their work: If one falls down, his friend can help him up. But pity the man who falls and has no one to help him up! Though one may be overpowered, two can defend themselves. . . . A cord of three strands is not quickly broken" (Ecclesiastes 4:9–10, 12).

According to Rick Warren (2012, 256), sanity is "wholeness of mind; making decisions based on the truth." However, Jesus is the only higher power who offers the truth. In John 14:6 (NIV), Jesus said, "I am the way and the truth and the life. No one comes to the Father except through me." As Christians, we are Jesus's followers, and all of our decisions must be made through Him. A successful marriage can be built based on the acronym SANITY. S stands for "strength," which is defined as "the quality that allows someone to deal with problems in a determined and effective way (*Merriam-Webster's* "2016, 829). Married life is not supposed to be consistently problematic; however, problems will occur from time to time. Certainly, if couples accept Jesus as their Lord and Savior, they will receive strength to face the issues that, in the past, might have caused them arguments and dissension. Now, when they face difficulty, they can say, "God is our refuge and strength, an ever-present help in trouble. Therefore, we shall not fear" (Psalm 46:1).

A stands for "acceptance." The apostle Paul instructs us, "Accept one another, then, just as Christ accepted you, in order to bring praise to God" (Romans 15:7 NIV). Only prayer can change an individual to be a better human being. When Christians pray, they must ask God to give them the ability to change what they can change and to accept the things they cannot change. The more we believe in Jesus Christ, the more faith we will have, which in turn will allow us to experience and dwell in His power. In this way, we will find it easier to accept others as they are, complete with faults and imperfections. However, with acceptance comes responsibility.

N stands for "new life." After the wedding, a couple begins a new life together because they have become one. They now face the task of learning how to do everything together: eat together, walk together, sleep together, and share everything together. The penalty of human sin was paid in full by Jesus on the cross. The hope of a new life brings freedom from bondage. When someone becomes a Christian, he becomes a brand-new person inside. He is not the same anymore. A new life has begun.

"Therefore, if anyone is in Christ, the new creation has come: The old has gone, the new life is here!" (2 Corinthians 5:17 NIV).

The letter *I* in our acronym stands for "integrity." Integrity is the quality of being honest and fair. A married couple builds integrity with each other as they follow through with their promises. Each starts trusting in what the other says. The apostle John placed great value on integrity: "Nothing brings me greater joy than hearing that my children are living in the truth" (3 John 4 NIV). Individuals must understand that a half-truth is a whole lie; moreover, a lie is the result of weakness and fear. Truth fears nothing except concealment. Truth often hurts, but it is the lie that leaves the scars. Men and women of integrity and courage are not afraid to tell the truth. Their courage comes from a power greater than man. As Jesus said to the disciples, "I am the way, the truth, and the life" (John 14:6).

The letter *T* stands for "trust." Trust is confidence placed in something or someone. When a couple learns to trust each other, the relationship, and Jesus, the marriage will succeed. "The fear of man bringeth a snare: but he who putteth his trust in the LORD shall be safe" (Proverbs 29:25). Also, "Then you will know the truth, and the truth will set you free" (John 8:32 KJV).

Although it is important for a couple to trust each other, it is even more important for them to trust in the Lord, admitting that their life together depends on Jesus and allowing Him to work for them. They must recognize they are powerless to change circumstances over which they have no control. As Psalm 46:10 reminds us, "Let go of your concerns! Then you will know that I am God. I rule the nations. I rule the earth." That choice is a battle because we all want to control our lives and make our own rules. But stress relief always starts with letting God be God. It always starts with saying, "God, I'm giving up control because you can control the things that are out of control in my life" (Warren 2012, 257).

The last letter in SANITY is *Y*, which stands for "you." Jesus Christ loves you the way you are (1 Corinthians 10:13). You do not have to measure up to a certain standard in order for Him to love you. In the book of Matthew, Jesus said, "Come unto me, all ye that labour and are heavy laden and I will give you rest. Take my yoke upon you, and learn of me; for I am meek and lowly in heart: and ye shall find rest unto your souls. For my yoke is easy, and my burden is light" (Matthew 11:28–30). Furthermore, Paul stated, "While we were still sinners, Christ died for us" (Romans 5:8 NIV).

People should not hesitate to get married, because God will help them to overcome any obstacles they will face. "And God is faithful; he will not let you be tempted beyond what you can bear. But when you are tempted, he will also provide a way out" (1 Corinthians 10:13 NIV). When a person accepts Jesus Christ as their personal Savior, that person is guaranteed both eternal life and God's protection in times of trial. As Nahum 1:7 says, "The Lord is good, a refuge in times of trouble. He cares for those who trust in him."

Let's go a little further with the word *trust*. Some of us drink Coca-Cola on a daily basis, and we really don't know what is inside the can; we simply trust it without a doubt. However, we struggle to trust in the truly important areas of life. For example, individuals may want to get married but worry that things may not go according to plan. But worrying about the future and being afraid of getting engaged will solve nothing. Worry gives way to anxiety or unease; in turn, this allows the mind to dwell on difficulty or troubles.

Many people worry about things over which they have no control. This demonstrates a lack of trust in God. As the psalmist David reminds us: "The Lord is my shepherd; I shall not want. He maketh me to lie down in green pastures: he leadeth me beside the still waters. He restoreth my soul: he leadeth me in the paths of righteousness for his name's sake" (Psalm 23:1–3). In conclusion, we may boldly say, "The Lord is my helper, and I will not fear what man shall do unto me" (Hebrews 13:6).

A man who decides to get married is a man who trusts in the Lord. Morals are extremely important. Morals are concerned with the principles of right and wrong behavior and the goodness or badness of human character. It seems, though, that the topic of morals scares some people. The word *moral* simply means honest. Honesty is the face of moral character, and it connotes positive and virtuous attributes such as integrity, truthfulness, and straightforwardness.

Success emphasizes personal responsibility. Instead of playing the "accuse and excuse" game of blame, it is better for a couple to face reality; it is better for everyone to face their poor choices and deal with what they can control. Of course, we cannot control all that happens to us, but we can control how we respond. This is the secret of a successful marriage.

After getting married, a couple needs to allow enough time to understand each other. As has been noted, they must stop wasting time blaming each other and instead use their energy to correct the problems that arise and make plans for a better future. Problems are an inevitable part of life. When we stop hiding our own faults and stop hurling accusations at others, then the healing power of Christ can begin working in our minds and emotions. This is the secret of happiness.

Even if individuals would like to get married and have a family, they may fear the difficulties that marriage will bring. Such people should stop worrying about things over which they have absolutely no control. Instead, they should seek the Lord for His guidance.

Prior to marriage, one element to consider is the level of education of the prospective spouses. If the gap is too wide, it is best to proceed with caution because differences in this area may elicit issues in the future. Naturally, education is important, because an educated person has greater opportunities for growth and promotion.

Age difference is another factor to consider. Although there may be no significant factors relating to an age gap between a husband and a wife, the age difference should still be taken into consideration. Large differences in age can lead to problems in the future. For instance, if the age gap is too wide, the marital relationship will likely sour in the long run. If a woman wants to marry a man who is twenty to thirty years older than she is, there are many questions to ask: Is it due to any coercion or compulsion (by elders in the church, through the use of power or intimidation by the man, because of poverty and subsequent insecurity of the woman, etc.)? Is it because of an illogical infatuation? Is it a calculated move by the woman to swindle his riches? Is it to obtain celebrity status? Unless there is a genuine bond of love and affection between the couple, a wide gap in age can lead to detrimental consequences in the end. There is always the danger of the marital bond deteriorating, leaving painful scars in its place.

The apostle Paul says, "Every one of you should know how to possess his vessel in sanctification and honor" (1 Thessalonians 4:4). It is important to understand the meaning of the term *sanctification*, for us as individuals and as marriage partners. The infinitive *to sanctify* literally means "to set apart" for special use or purpose; it signifies something that is made holy or sacred" (Martin 1964, 736). Sanctification is regularly associated with the Christian life. A Christian life is a holy life. Paul asked the Christians of Rome to offer their lives as a holy sacrifice: "I beseech you therefore, brethren, by the mercies of God, that ye present your bodies a living sacrifice, holy, acceptable unto God, which is your reasonable service" (Romans 12:1). The word *sacrifice* speaks of the sacrifice of Christ, which means that we cannot do what the Holy Spirit demands unless our faith is placed strictly in Christ and the cross. This then gives the Holy Spirit latitude to carry out this great work within our lives (Swaggart 1993, 1993). "Elect according to the foreknowledge of God the Father, through sanctification of the Spirit, unto obedience and sprinkling of the blood of Jesus Christ: grace unto you, and peace, be multiplied" (1 Peter 1:2).

God is the only one who can impart holiness and sanctification in someone's life. The long history of His efforts to redeem humanity, culminating in Jesus Christ, is an expression of His desire to sanctify men, to set them apart for His purposes. "The teachings of the New Testament compel us to view sanctification in a double aspect: it is accomplished not through achievement of moral perfection, but in the perfection of the gift of the Holy Spirit" (Martin 1964, 736). Sanctification is a real transformation, not just the appearance of one. God calls His children to holiness, and He graciously gives what He commands.

To those individuals who are opposed to getting married, it is fine not to get married. But if you are not going to marry, you should not be planning on having sexual intercourse, either. That's where sanctification comes in. The Bible says, "No man can serve two masters: for either he will hate the one, and love the other; or else he will hold to the one, and despise the other. Ye cannot serve God and mammon" (Matthew 6:24 KJV). The apostle explained it clearly in the book of 1 Corinthians: "Now concerning the things whereof ye wrote unto me: It is good for a man not to touch a woman. Nevertheless, to avoid fornication, let every man have his own wife, and let every woman have her own husband" (1 Corinthians 7:1–2 KJV). In addition, for those who oppose getting married, "But if they cannot contain, let them marry: for it is better to marry than to burn" (1 Corinthians 7:9 KJV).

Marriage is a big commitment, and according to Genesis 2:18, marriage is an institution created by God Himself. It is normal to be a little uneasy before moving into marriage, but always remember that God is love: "Whoever does not love does not know God" (1 John 4:8). Bible says, "God is not a man that he should lie; neither the son of man that he should repent: hath he said, and shall he not do it? Or hath he spoken, and shall he not make it good?" (Numbers 23:19 KJV). God designed marriage to be the most intimate of human relationships, but such intimacy cannot be obtained without wholesome responsibility and communication (Chapman, 2003, 35). God created marriage, and He will surely support it as long as the marriage stands according to His will.

There is nothing wrong with delaying marriage while waiting for something good to happen. Marriage is a lifetime commitment. It is well worth it to wait for the right person. Sometimes, while waiting for an answer from God, individuals may begin to lose faith. The silence from God can be deafening. People can easily lose patience, even in their prayers. However, we can see in God's Word that time and time again, He has called upon His children to wait on Him. The Bible said that Abraham waited until he was one hundred years old for his promise to be fulfilled (Genesis 21:5). Joshua marched around the walls of Jericho and waited for seven days before God brought the walls down (Joshua 6:20). Daniel waited to be delivered in the lions' den (Daniel 6). Israel waited for their Messiah to come. Mary waited nine months for Jesus to be born. Instead of opposing marriage or rushing into it, wait on God in prayer, because the Bible says, "Pray without ceasing" (Philippians 4 KJV).

Chapter 10: A Supportive Couple

To describe a submissive wife and how she is to act toward her husband: "Likewise, ye wives, be in subjection to your own husbands; that, if any obey not the word, they also may without the word be won by the conversation of the wives" (1 Peter 3:1 KJV). He knew that if a man married an unsupportive wife, he would have a difficult time achieving success in his marriage. Remember, Peter was a married man before he was called to be an apostle. The Bible says that Jesus visited Peter's house and performed a miracle on behalf of Peter's mother-in-law (Matthew 8:14). Peter, as a married man, was well qualified to talk about a supportive wife, being the head of a household and understanding the duties that entailed.

God has given a clear message in the Bible outlining the husband as the head of the home (Ephesians 5:22). Each man is unique; therefore, each home is unique. Nonetheless, every man is expected to govern or to lead, though each may do it differently. On the other hand, God created each woman to be a helper for her husband (Courtney 2013, 56).

One of the biggest reasons many marriages end in divorce is very simple: couples do not find out their mates' likes or dislikes before taking their vows and thus do not know how to support each other. Couples need to discover how to be a supportive mate prior to the wedding day, and they need to understand the biblical guidelines that foster a happy home. The biblical principles applied in Genesis 2:18 are clear and still relevant today. The marriage sacrament will not be successful unless these principles are applied accordingly. They are as follows:

1. God created wives to be helpers to their husbands (Genesis 2:18).
2. God commands wives to respect their husbands (Ephesians 5:33).
3. God commissions husbands to be the leaders of their homes (Ephesians 5:22–24).
4. God commands husbands to love their wives (Ephesians 5:25).

The first principle is that God created woman to be her husband's helper. Genesis 2:18 says that when God created Eve, she was created to be a "helper for him [Adam]." However, a woman being a man's helper doesn't always sound great in today's liberated world. It is a hard statement for even some Christians to swallow. But the fact is this is a quality of a good wife. When a wife acts as a helper fit for her husband, she is commited to her wifely duties. When a wife acts as a supportive helper, she is glorifying God because women were created to be their husbands' helpers. Certainly, this is a tough thing for a modern woman to accept (Courtney 2013, 57). As a believer, though, each wife must comply with the Word of God by supporting her husband. Even if things were not done accordingly before, it is never too late for a wife to start doing what is right.

The second principle is that wives are to respect their husbands: "Wives, respect and obey your husbands in the same way. Then the husbands who do not obey the word of God will want to know God. They will want to know God because their wives live good lives, even though they say nothing about God" (1 Peter 3:1 KJV). Respect and support are intertwined and equally important in a marriage. If a wife respects her husband, she will surely support him also. According to the Bible, to be a servant is not a bad thing. Of being a servant, Jesus said to His disciples, "Whoever desires to become great among you, let him be your servant" (Matthew 20:26). In the same manner, a wife must become a servant to her husband if she desires to help him fulfill his responsibilities as the head of the household. According to Dr. Emerson (2004, 17), a wife is called to respect and support even an unloving husband.

The third principle is for husbands to be the leaders of their homes (Ephesians 5:22). A leader is someone who has followers. God gave the husband the authority to rule over his wife and lead her (Genesis 3:16). This means that a husband needs the support of his wife in order to perform his duties and fulfill his responsibilities. This is what the Bible tells us about leaders: " Let every soul be subject unto the higher powers. For there is no power but God: the powers that be are ordained of God. Whosoever therefore resisteth the power, resisteth the ordinance of God: and they that resist shall receive to themselves damnation" (Romans 13:1–2 KJV).

According to Debi Pearl (2010), men are created to be God's helpers. Jesus willingly became a helper to the Father, and the Holy Spirit became a helper to the Son. Society is structured so that men and women must submit to authorities like government, employers, police officers, the Internal Revenue Service, child protection agencies, the courts, and so on. There is no loss of dignity in subordination when it serves a higher purpose. In similar fashion, God made each wife to be a helpmeet to her husband so that she could bolster his ambitions, making him more productive and efficient at whatever he chooses to do. However, the wife is not on the board of directors with an equal vote. She has no authority to set the agenda, but if a husband trusts his wife enough, he will consult her as a personal advisor (Pearl 2010, 23).

The fourth principle is God's command to husbands to love their wives (Ephesians 5:25). No matter the attitude or the condition of the wife, God commands the husband to love her: "Husbands, love your wives, even as Christ also loved the church, and gave himself for it" (Ephesians 5:25 KJV). A husband is called to love even a disrespectful wife, just as a wife is called to respect even an unloving husband. There is no justification for a husband to say, "I will love my wife after she respects me" (Emerson 2004, 16). The Bible never says that Jesus loves the church because the church is perfect. Jesus loves an imperfect church.

Peter was a fisherman, and he was also a married man when Jesus chose him to be an apostle (Matthew 4:18). He knew about married life from personal experience and recognized the importance of having a supportive wife. Because of his real-life experience, he was the perfect man to talk about the value of a supportive wife. Like every other human being, Peter needed support from others in order to achieve success. Support has been defined as "to agree with and give encouragement to someone, to endure, to bring to a place, to keep from failing" (*Webster's New World Dictionary* 2016, 1345). This is what every man needs from his wife.

Peter addressed wives on how to be a blessing to their husbands, how to stand behind them and support them. He knew that one of the greatest needs of a husband is to have a supportive wife. For example, after a man has had a long day at work, he expects his wife to appreciate and support his efforts. He will not welcome a wife who nags, complains, and grumbles about everything he doesn't do right. In fact, her behavior can have a very negative effect on him and their marriage. If he is already overworked, he certainly doesn't want to come home to a wife who is tearing him down instead of building him up. He desires a wife who positions herself under her husband's authority, which is God's order for their home. A good wife should always support her husband's decisions. "From the beginning, God meant for woman to be a comfort, a blessing, a reward, a friend, an encouragement, and a right-hand woman" (Pearl 2010, 94). Also, "A wise woman sets a joyful mood in her home. Through laughter, music, and happy times, she creates a positive attitude in her children. She knows that a lighthearted home relieves her husband's success" (33).

In the book of Esther, a terrible incident involving Queen Vashti occurred. King Ahasuerus held a feast, and at the conclusion of the seven-day festivities, he called for Queen Vashti to appear before him in order to show off her beauty. Unfortunately, Queen Vashti refused and did not come before the king and his guests. She failed the king in public, showing great disrespect (Esther 1:11). Understandably, King Ahasuerus was furious with the queen and very upset in the presence of his guests. The seven princes of Persia and Media said to the wise men, "What shall we do unto Queen Vashti according to the law, because she hath not performed the commandment of King Ahasuerus by the chamberlains?" (Esther 1:15 KJV).

The queen was not only disobedient to the king, but she also violated the law of Xerxes. Unfortunately, there was a royal commandment from the king that was written among the laws of the Persians and the Medes that allowed King Ahasuerus to dismiss Vashti and find another queen (Esther 1:19). This law could not be altered. A man who occupied such a high position in government needed a supportive wife who cooperated with him. One can imagine how the king felt after his wife turned him down in front of all of his very important guests. The queen's disobedience was aimed not only at the king, but also at his guests and the other women in the country. She did not set a good example, so an example had to be made of her.

Even though the New Testament was not written yet, one can see that the queen was not in accord with the book of Ephesians: "Wives, submit yourselves unto your own husbands, as unto the Lord" (Ephesians 5:22 KJV). Every wife should respect her spouse's personal decisions and become the shoulder to lean on when he needs support. She should work with him to maintain balance in his life.

The role of the wife in the marriage relationship can be confusing, so how can a wife support her husband effectively? It is wise for her to go to the Scriptures to see exactly what God has said of her role. From the beginning, she was designed to be a helpmate to man: "And the LORD God said, It is not good that the man should be alone; I will make a help meet for him" (Genesis 2:18 KJV). It seems, however, that Queen Vashti was confused. She may have had what she thought was a valid reason not to appear before the king, but it was not in accord with either God's law or the law of man.

Some women believe that the word *submission* is a tool used by men to manipulate and control their wives. But if submission is understood biblically, a man will understand that he cannot use the principle in order to manipulate his wife (1 Peter 3:1). It is very important for each wife and husband to understand that when the apostle Peter commandes a woman to submit to her own husband, he is not recommending that she become a doormat for her husband to take advantage of. Instead, Peter urges each wife to take her place as her husband's chief supporter and helper according to what is written: "I will make a help meet for him" (Genesis 2:18 KJV). According to Rick Renner (2003, 741), God never designed a wife to assume authority over her husband. Otherwise, the Bible would not say, "For the husband is the head of the wife, even as Christ is the head of the church: and he is the saviour of the body" (Ephesians 5:23 KJV).

When a woman honors her husband, she honors God. When a woman obeys her husband, she obeys God. The degree to which a woman reverences her husband is the same degree to which she reverences the Creator, and as she serves her husband, she serves God. In the same way, when a woman dishonors her husband, she dishonors God (Pearl 2010, 22).

Concerning marriage, the Bible declares, "Wives, submit to your own husbands, as to the Lord. For the husband is the head of the wife, as Christ is the head of the church; and he is the saviour of the body. Therefore, just as the church is subject to Christ, so let the wives be to their own husbands in everything" (Ephesians 5:22–24 KJV). Submission creates a chain of command, harmony, and order to any organization, including the family of God.

God has ordained submission between the three persons of the Trinity, and He has ordained submission within marriage. Paul made this clear when he taught, "I want you to know that the head of every man is Christ, the head of woman is man, and the head of Christ is God" (1 Corinthians 11:3). Furthermore, there is one head in our government and in most organizations. Therefore, it stands to reason that there should be one head in the family. When a woman is submissive and supportive of her own husband, it eliminates a power struggle between the two and brings great harmony to the relationship.

The role of the wife is clearly described in the Bible. Although a husband and a wife are equal in their relationship in Christ, their specific roles operate differently in marriage. For example, Titus instructed the older women to train the younger women to love their husbands and their children, to be self-controlled and pure, to be busy at home, to be kind, and to be subject to their husbands so that no one would malign the Word of God (Titus 2:4–5 KJV). "When a weak sister fulfills her divine purpose of being a true help meet, it brings great glory and joy to God" (Pearl 2010, 44).

The book of Ruth relates a beautiful story about a young widow named Ruth who supported her mother-in-law, Naomi. The story begins with a family from Bethlehem who left their country because of a great famine and took refuge in another country, Moab. In this family were four members: Elimelech, the father; Naomi, his wife; and their two sons, Mahlon and Chilion. After a number of years, "Elimelech, Naomi's husband, died; and she was left, and her two sons" (Ruth 1:3). After the death of their father, the sons married two women from Moab: Orpah, and Ruth, and they dwelt in Moab for approximately ten years (Ruth 1:4).

Sadly, both of Naomi's sons then died, which left Naomi with her two daughters-in-law. Naomi asked the pair to return to their parents because she did not have any other sons to offer them. According to the custom of the day, if a brother died, a younger brother could marry his widow. Naomi asked her two daughters-in-laws this question: "Are there yet any more sons in my womb, that they may be your husbands?" (Ruth 1:11 KJV). Furthermore, in the book of Matthew, a Sadducee referenced this practice, saying, "If a man die, having no children, his brother shall marry his wife, and raise up seed unto his brother" (Matthew 22:24 KJV).

After some discussion about the situation, Orpah wept and kissed Naomi good-bye, returning to her family as a young widow. The Bible does not say that Orpah did anything wrong when she left Naomi. She simply realized there was nothing left for her. Her husband had died, and she didn't have a child; she did not have any other choice but to return to her family.

When we have positive input, we also have a positive output, and when we have negative input, we have negative output (Zig Ziglar 1985, 25). Ruth had positive input from her time spent in Naomi's family; then, when circumstances changed, she was committed to her mother-in-law and went the extra mile for her. Ruth's approach was different from Orpah's; she did not consider herself, but rather considered Naomi. Ruth showed compassion for Naomi and expressed her deep feelings for her. Ruth was a supportive daughter-in-law and became deeply attached to her mother-in-law. This was evidenced by her words to Naomi: "Intreat me not to leave thee, or to return from following after thee: for whither thou goest, I will go; and where thou lodgest, I will lodge: thy people shall be my people, and thy God my God: where thou diest, will I die, and there will I be buried: the Lord do so to me, and more also, if ought but death part thee and me" (Ruth 1:16–17 KJV).

Ruth modeled the truth of Philippians 2:4 (KJV): "Look not every man on his own things, but every man also on the things of others." This is an example of the kind of support husbands should receive from their wives.

The book of Malachi talks about another important element of a good marriage: companionship. Husbands and wives who spend time together as companions develop a strong and meaningful friendship. Without true friendship and companionship, however, couples will not support each other in their deepest needs. In marriage, couples make a covenant promise to be supportive of each other for the rest of their lives. The prophet Malachi warned men to treat their wives in a righteous and loving manner "because the LORD has been witness between you and the wife of your youth, with whom you have dealt treacherously; yet she is your companion and your wife by covenant" (Malachi 2:14).

Everyone in a family needs support, including the children. Husbands and wives should support each other, but they must not neglect this need of their children as well. A father who supports his child goes to the child's basketball games, and a mother who supports her child helps with the child's homework. Ultimately, it is very important for all the members of a family to support one another.

A wife needs to let her husband know that she understands her role in the family and desires to show her respect and support of him. In turn, the husband should acknowledge his acceptance of his role in the family and his intention to love his wife and children. Of course, this does not happen automatically. Therefore, the couple needs to identify the obstacles that could hinder the success of their marriage. In any family where two or more people are involved, there will always be discussions and conflicts about each person's responsibilities.

According to Ziglar (1985, 48), "One of the best opportunities for teaching moral values and responsibility lies in the daily functioning of the home." The mental outlook of the couple, whether positive or negative, comes into play here. According to Ziglar (1985, 58), positive thinking makes room for positive actions; likewise, negative thinking leads to negative actions. Positive thinking will allow both spouses to become more effective in the use of their abilities within the marriage. For a wife to become an excellent and supportive wife, she must maintain a positive attitude toward her role as a helper to her husband; only then will she become a woman of virtue and excellence. King Solomon knew how important this was, saying, "An excellent wife is the crown of her husband, but she who causes shame is like rottenness in his bones" (Proverbs 12:4). A positive wife will encourage her husband in a positive way. When people do more than they are supposed to do, by going the extra mile, eventually they will gain more than what they ever anticipated (48).

Chapter 11: The Little Things Married Couples Should Know

There are many things married couples should know in order to ensure a lifetime of happiness. When two individuals enter into marriage, they are about to begin one of the most important phases of their lives. Marriage is the institution that God created in order to reproduce human beings on earth (Genesis 2:18).

"Marriage is a system by means of which persons who are sinful and contentious are so caught up by a dream and purpose bigger than themselves that they work through the years, in spite of repeated disappointments, to make the dream come true" (Wright and Roberts 1997, 6). Marriage is more than a set of rules and roles. The couple must work to discover who does what and when. There must be some division of labor in order to create balance. The couple must find a way to discover who has the capability and giftedness in specific areas within the family.

Paul explains how the Holy Spirit works in everyone differently for the glory of God:

Now there are diversities of gifts, but the same Spirit. And there are differences of administrations, but the same Lord. And there are diversities of operations, but it is the same God which worketh all in all.

But the manifestation of the Spirit is given to every man to profit withal. For to one is given by the Spirit the word of wisdom; to another the word of knowledge by the same Spirit; to another faith by the same Spirit; to another the gifts of healing by the same Spirit; to another the working of miracles; to another prophecy; to another discerning of spirits; to another divers kinds of tongues; to another the interpretation of tongues: but all these worketh that one and the selfsame Spirit, dividing to very man severally as he will. (1 Corinthians 12:5–11)

Headship and submission are two areas that usually create tension for many couples. Tension is defined as a state in which people, groups, countries, and so on disagree with and feel anger toward each other (*Merriam-Webster's* 2016). It is normal for married couples to feel tense at times. However, husbands and wives can work through this together. As Wright says (2012, 125), "A really good marriage has the feel of a man and woman blended together into natural movement where individuality is obviously present, but really isn't the point, something perhaps like dance partners of many years who anticipate each other's steps with practice."

After a marriage begins, neither party loses identity. However, it takes communication to share both individuals' identities and their identity as a couple. Communication is like the process of breathing; without it, the couple cannot stay alive (Chapman 2003, 43). Communication is defined as the "act or process of using words, sounds, signs, or behaviors to express or exchange information or to express ideas, thoughts, feelings, etc., to someone else" (*Merriam-Webster's* 2016, 282). Furthermore, "Communication is a plan or design for changing human behavior on a large-scale through the transfer of new ideas" (Rogers 1973).

Intimacy is something human beings gain and hopefully retain forever. Married couples do not obtain intimacy and put it in a safe box. It is fluid and directly related to their quality of communication (Rogers 1973, 43). Accordingly, communication is a vital component of marriage and builds a sense of intimacy and identity as a couple. "Communication serves as the process by which family members create and share their meanings with each other. Members develop a relational culture—or a shared worldview—that contributes to creating a relatively unique communication system" (Galvin 2008, 3).

According to Chapman (2003, 58), more couples are living together for longer periods of time. Understanding the communication of these couples provides us with important insights into their marital relationships. In marriage, communication alone is not enough; it must be healthy in order to be effective.

"Just as breathing toxic fumes are able to lead a human being to death, so unhealthy communication patterns can actually destroy the marriage. Some communication patterns are positive, leading the couples to intimacy in the marriage. But many communication patterns are negative, leading married couples apart rather than together" (Chapman 2003, 43). Likewise, great communication means that the couple is experiencing intimacy.

God's solution to our innate fear of rejection is based on Christ's sacrificial payment for our sins. Through this payment, we find forgiveness, reconciliation, and total acceptance through Christ. Reconciliation means that those who were enemies have become friends. The apostle Paul describes a believer's transformation from enemy to friendship with God: "Once you were alienated from God and were enemies in your minds because of your evil behavior. But now he has reconciled you by Christ's physical body through death to present you holy in his sight, without blemish and free from accusation" (Colossians 1:21–22). Jesus also said, "I no longer call you servants, because a servant does not know his master's business. Instead, I have called you friends, for everything that I learned from my Father I have made known to you" (John 15:15 NIV). When we find acceptance in Christ, it is easier to extend acceptance in marriage.

"Marriage is a relationship between a man and a woman intended by God to be a monogamous relationship" (Wright 2012, 6). "The family is one of the foundational social institutions in all societies, although the definition of the family varies from place to place and from time to time. The married couple generally forms the nucleus of the family" (Waite 2005, 87). Marriage is intended to be a permanent bond in which many needs—the need for someone to love and to be loved, the need for deep friendship, for allowance, for children, for companionship, for sexual satisfaction, and the need to escape loneliness—are satisfied (Wright 2012, 6). Furthermore, marriage ought to be a bond of love reflecting the love Christ has for His people—a bond of sacrificial love where a husband and a wife have become one, one flesh, a unity (Wright, 2012, p. 6).

There are three main reasons why people get married: (1) for procreation, (2) to avoid fornication, and (3) to avoid loneliness. First, people marry to have children. "So God created mankind in his own image, in the image of God he created them; male and female he created them" (Genesis 1:27 NIV). The concept of being made in God's image, meaning that human beings are able to enter into relationship with God and God's creatures, is empowering. It suggests that the Old Testament's view of human nature is far more positive than our dour emphasis on human sinfulness has led us to imagine (Genesis 1:26–28). Married couples should take the time to show that they truly care for each other in every way. Usually this produces children, an outward manifestation of the couple's love.

The second reason for individuals to marry is to avoid fornication. "Fornication is defined as voluntary sexual intercourse between two unmarried persons or two persons not married to each other" (Martin 1964, 263). The apostle Paul said, "Now concerning the things whereof ye wrote unto me: It is good for a man not to touch a woman. Nevertheless, to avoid fornication, let every man have his own wife, and let every woman have her own husband" (1 Corinthians 7:1–2). Marriage allows for a man and a woman to fulfill their sexual needs in the way God intended (Wright 2012, 8).

The third reason a man and a woman get married is to avoid loneliness. God, the creator of the universe, said, "It is not good that the man should be alone" (Genesis 2:18). Everyone who marries enters the marriage relationship with certain expectations. These expectations arise from many sources, including parents, family values, society, books, and our own ideas. "If you're considering marriage, you must have some hopes and dreams about it" (Wright 2012, 6). It is important to take the time to find out what these expectations are, which of them can be achieved, how they can be achieved, and how to handle expectations when circumstances do not go according to plan. The word *expectation* carries with it the attitude of hope. Hope has been defined as the anticipation of something good. Hope is necessary because it motivates human beings and keeps people going (Wright 2012, 6). There are many types of expectations, some spoken and some unspoken.

"God is so passionate about marriage that He put a lot of emphasis on it throughout the Bible" (Smalley and Smalley 2015, 1). The Scriptures are rampant with verses about marriage. For example, "It is not good for man to be alone. I will make a helper suitable for him" (Genesis 2:18). "It is recommended in the Scriptures to be honorable among all, and therefore marriage is not to be entered

into unadvisedly or lightly, but reverently, discreetly, advisedly, soberly and in the fear of God" (*Nelson's Minister's Manual*, 2003, 14).

Certainly, not all men are the same, and this affects their behavior in marriage. According to Debi Pearl (2010, 75), there are three kinds of men:

Jesus was the perfect balance.
Some men have a little of all three,
but one type tends to be dominant.

For instance, some men are freely givers to their wives. They never get tired of taking care of their spouses. They give because they enjoy it, and they get pleasure from making their wives happy. This is one type of man.

There are other men, who also give, but they do not really care if their wives are happy or not.

Some man is just like a woomate with their wives, their wives must share everething with them, and they will share the bill 50% regardeless if the wife works or not.

It seems that God made each male to express one side of His three natures. No single man expresses a well-rounded image of God; it is impossible to find one man who embodies all three types equally at the same time (Pearl 2010, 75). Sadly, some men do not pay attention to the details that would make a strong marriage; they only expect to have a memorable journey.

According to Smalley and Smalley (2015, 5), shortly after the wedding ceremony, most couples begin to see faults in their spouses that they previously overlooked. Some then become disappointed. However, when couples work together, they help each other succeed. The best practice of marriage is teamwork. Couples need to remain connected in every way to maintain this sense of team. "If a marriage is between two servants, it will be increasingly uniting and satisfying both in and out of the bedroom" (Driscoll and Driscoll 2012, 160).

Another one of the little things that can help couples grow together is the knowledge of sex. According to Courtney Joseph (2013, 109), "Sex is a basic physical and emotional need men have." God designed men this way. It is a good thing. Not only do they need sex often, but their wives need to know that their husbands are desirable for sex. Likewise, husbands need to know that their wives are desirable for sex (109).

Married couples can do many little things to show their appreciation for their mate. For example, they can make breakfast for each other and share it while in bed. Such gestures can make a partner feel important, like a king or a queen. A woman has absolutely nothing to lose when she makes her husband feel he is an important member of the household, and it is actually quite easy to do. For example, she can ask him if he needs anything when she is planning to go to the store. In this way, she shows that she cares for him. Although such actions may seem trivial, they can make all the difference in a successful marriage. This, of course, goes both ways. A wife must feel that her husband values her participation in the marriage. According to Michael Pearl (2012, 39), a wife has more faith in a man who includes her in the decision-making process. "When she is shut out, she feels at the mercy of a fallible man, who doesn't have her best interests at heart."

A wife should always respect her husband, no matter what. Ephesians 5:33 says, "However, each one of you also must love his wife as he loves himself, and the wife must respect her husband." Since God commands that wives respect their husbands, we must define what this means and understand how it is evidenced through a couple's actions. *Respect* in Ephesians 5:33 means reverence, awe, honor, and esteem. Respect is an attitude displayed through one's actions.

A woman should respect her husband's knowledge, opinions, and decisions. Furthermore, she should not criticize him or expect the worst of his actions. That is not respect; that is discouragement. She should respect his desire to work and protect him, and allow him to lead, letting him know that she respects his hard work. She might also express that she feels more secure when he is home and that she is grateful he protects the family. According to Dr. Emerson Eggerichs (2004, 16), no husband will feel fond affection and love in his heart when he believes his wife has contempt for who he is as a human being. Ironically, the deepest need of the wife to feel loved is undermined when she disrespects her husband.

Proverbs 31:10–12 paints a picture of a woman who loves and honors her husband: "Who can find a virtuous woman? For her price is far above rubies. The heart of her husband doth safely trust in her, so that he shall have no need of spoil. And he will have no lack of gain. She does him good, and not harm, all the days of her life."

Likewise, the husband should daily show his wife how much he loves her. The Bible instructs the husband to love his wife as Christ loves His church (Ephesians 5:25). A man can please his wife by taking a few minutes to mop the kitchen floor, offer her a night off from household responsibilities, or help the children complete their homework. Some husbands are good cooks and show love to their wives by cooking dinner. These acts may seem minor, but they can make a big difference in a marriage. In addition, a man should make his wife feel loved. For example, King Solomon said, "Let him kiss me with the kisses of his mouth: for thy love is better than wine" (Song of Solomon 1:2(KJV).

Seemingly insignificant acts can make all the difference in a relationship. If one spouse sees that the other is feeling a little sad, he or she should speak words of encouragement. Sympathy is feeling sorrow for your mate, pitying him or her, but empathy is feeling sorrow with your mate. It is good for spouses to feel empathy. Lastly, husbands and wives must speak aloud and say "I love you," calling each other by name. This shows understanding, sympathy, and awareness of each other's feelings.

According to Paul, a word of wisdom is important when talking to a mate: "One is given by the Spirit the word of wisdom; to another the word of knowledge by the same Spirit" (1 Corinthians 12:8 KJV). Wisdom speaks for itself; it has the power to uplift. Instead of putting one's spouse down, it is better to speak words of wisdom.

In a marriage, both partners may have to do certain things they would rather not do. For example, a wife may not like to cook, but in order to keep her family fed, she might have to learn how to cook. Likewise, a husband may not know how to cook, but if cooking will make his wife happy, it is preferable to learn how to cook. Husband and wife must manage the responsibility to take the trash out on a daily basis, or even more than once a day if necessary. No one enjoys this task, but it must be done. All married couples will have conflict. Conflict cannot be avoided because marriage is an unconditional commitment to an imperfect person (Driscoll and Driscoll 2012, 86). However, by sharing responsibilities, couples will minimize conflict and promote harmony.

Anger must be avoided because it is one of the most destructive emotions known to mankind. It can take many forms, when one permits it to dominate. It has the power to destroy any family—rich or poor, black or white. It ruined the first family, causing the first murder when Cain flew into a rage and killed his brother, Abel. Since then, it has ruined millions of lives, marriages, friendships, and other relationships (LaHaye 2005, 123).

Anger can squelch the richer emotion of love. Additionally, anger toward a person or situation can be displaced onto a loved one and wreak havoc on the relationship. Scripture warns men, "Love your wives and do not be bitter toward them" (Colossians 3:19). It is almost impossible to love someone and indulge in bitterness at the same time; holding on to bitterness will change the love to hate. The moment a couple starts hating each other, their love will vanish. Instead of enjoying their lives together, they will carry each other as a burden everywhere they go. Instead of loving each other, they will become slaves to each other.

Resentment produces stress and a release of destructive hormones in the human body and mind. It is not easy forget the bad things one's spouse has said or done; harsh words and thoughtless acts are indelibly etched in the memory. But resentment is a powerful tool that can destroy a marriage because it undermines the best qualities upon which a marriage should be built, including love, trust, and loyalty. "Resentment is a form of bondage that we can live without" (LaHaye 2005, 128). The Bible says, "Put away from yourselves every kind of malicious bitterness" (Ephesians 4:31 KJV).

Chapter 12: Family Work-Life Balance

Family work-life balance is a very important aspect for the success of a family. In order to build a successful family, work-life balance must be a top priority. Work is important because the Bible says, "For even when we were with you, we gave you this rule: 'The one who is unwilling to work shall not eat'" (2 Thessalonians 3:10 NIV). After the fall of man in the Garden of Eden, God blessed Adam and Eve and said to them, "Be fruitful and increase in number; fill the earth and subdue it. Rule over the fish in the sea and the birds in the sky and over every living creature that moves on the ground" (Genesis 1:28 NIV). Adam and Eve received an assignment from the Creator to work very hard in order to fulfill their responsibilities.

Work is very important. Both men and women must work hard to earn wages to raise their families. However, when work is overemphasized, instead of creating success for the family, it becomes a deterrent. An overworked person may not have enough time to spend with his or her family.

The Bible says, "Then God blessed the seventh day and made it holy, because on it he rested from all the work of creating that he had done" (Genesis 2:3 NIV). This verse authorizes family members to work and then rest. Rest is a must, and it is indispensable for a family to be successful. Without proper rest, the family will ultimately break down. In the New Testament, Jesus often asked His disciples to go with Him to a quiet place and rest: "Then, because so many people were coming and going that they did not even have a chance to eat, he said to them, 'Come with me by yourselves to a quiet place and get some rest'" (Mark 6:31 NIV). Jesus knew that after His disciples had rested, they would be better able to perform their duties. Jesus understood the importance of rest.

Rest is defined as "ceasing work or movement in order to relax, refresh oneself, or recover strength: needing to rest after a feverish activity." Resting is further defined as "an instance or period of relaxing or ceasing to engage in strenuous or stressful activity" (*Webster's New World Dictionary* 2016, 1144). There are many verses in the Bible that talk about resting. For example, in Psalm 127, Solomon said, "In vain you rise early and stay up late, toiling for food to eat—for he grants sleep to those he loves" (verse 2, NIV).

Work-life balance This article reviews aspects of contemporary theory and research on work-life balance. It starts by exploring why work-life balance has become an important topic for research and policy in some countries and after outlining traditional perspectives examines the concept of balance and its implications for the study of the relationship between work and the rest of life. A model outlining the causes, nature and consequences of a more or less acceptable work-life balance is presented and recent research is cited to illustrate its various dimensions. Finally, the topic is linked to the field of work and organizational psychology and a number of theoretical and conceptual issues of relevance to research in Europe are raised. (Guest 2002, 10).

True success is never an easy achievement. Happy and fulfilling marriages are products of extreme effort and follow a road that has been planned with success in mind. Communication in a marriage is the lifeblood of the relationship (Wright 2012, 202). If there is no work-life balance in a marriage, there will be no communication; and once communication is gone, the relationship is well on the way to being over. Sadly, it is quite common for a partner not to realize that the communication in the relationship is failing until it is too late (Wright 2012, 202).

In America one marriage out of three breaks down. In some parts of the country, it is one out of two. But where the family attends church regularly, the ratio is only one of forty. And if the family not only goes to church, but has a daily devotional life and family prayer, the ratio of divorce is only one in four hundred marriages. (Brecheen, 3)

Many Bible verses talk about family unity. The apostle Paul explains the family hierarchy in the book of Ephesians; however, it is impossible to have a family that conforms to this pattern if there is no work-life balance. Ephesians 6:2–4 (NLT) says: "'Honor your father and mother.' This is the first commandment with a promise: If you honor your father and mother, 'things will go well for you, and you will have a long life on the earth.' Fathers, do not provoke your children to anger by the way you treat them. Rather, bring them up with the discipline and instruction that comes from the Lord." How can these priorities be accomplished if there is no family time?

In the book of Proverbs, King Solomon instructs parents how to raise their children. For example, he says, "Train up a child in the way he should go; even when he is old he will not depart from it" (Proverbs 22:6). Paul explained to Timothy, in regard to caring for his household, that "he must manage his own household well, with all dignity keeping his children submissive" (1 Timothy 3:4). According to Dr. Brecheen (2001, 33), a definition of marriage is "someone to talk to, someone to touch, someone to be unified with, someone to raise kids with, someone to hurt with, someone to have fun with, someone to be serious with, someone to know inside and out, someone to need me, someone to love and someone to grow old with." This is attained only with a proper work-life balance.

Hilaire Louis Jean

What Is Success?

The simple definition of success is "achieving wealth, respect, or fame" (*Merriam-Webster's* 2016, 763). "Although success originally referred to any positive outcome, it has become increasingly associated with wealth and prestige" (*Oxford English Dictionary* 1971, 1337).

If a couple gets married but is unsuccessful in their marriage, it would have been better had they not gotten engaged in the first place. It is a waste of time to get married and not be committed to doing whatever it takes to be successful at it. It takes commitment and discipline to balance work and life in the context of marriage. According to Bill Butterworth. (Butterworth 2006, 17). Sometimes the wife may feel neglected. Maybe her husband has not been home before ten o'clock not even one night in the last several weeks, and she is lonely because her husband is always at work. Some jobs, unfortunately, require their employees to work half a day on Saturdays, but this is certainly not ideal.

The Bible says, "It is not good that the man should be alone; I will make him a help meet for him" (Genesis 2:18). This verse means that both men and women need companionship. "Therefore, shall a man leave his father and his mother, and shall cleave unto his wife: and they shall be one flesh" (Genesis 2:24 KJV). When Scripture speaks of cleaving, the idea in the Hebrew is to cling, hold, or keep close. The two are joined together, face-to-face, becoming one flesh. "In all creation, only human beings are sexually intimate face to face" (Eggerichs 2004, 125). Cleaving, however, is more than sexual. It also means spiritual and emotional closeness. The Bible describes a woman looking for closeness in the Song of Solomon: "When I found the one my heart loves, I held him and would not let him go till I had brought him to my mother's house" (Song of Solomon 3:4 NIV).

Nonetheless, sex is an important component of a successful marriage, especially to the man. It is "a basic physical and emotional need that men have. God designed men this way. Make sex a priority. Plan to have it.

Don't let life get so busy that you neglect this area in your marriage" (Joseph 2013, 108). "Defraud ye not one the other, except it be with consent for a time, that ye may give yourselves to fasting and prayer; and come together again, that Satan tempt you not for your incontinency" (1 Corinthians 7:5 KJV). It is important to know that if there is no work-life balance, sex will probably be neglected as well.

Much like a company that is depending on its sales team to follow certain guidelines to close a deal, a good marriage requires certain steps to be successful. A client may need extra hand-holding in order to seal the deal (Butterworth, 2006, 17), and spouses may need special attention. It's all about priorities. Some married men are more focused on tasks, and some are more focused on relationships. Ecclesiastes 9:7–9 (KJV) sums it up well:

Go thy way, eat thy bread with joy, and drink thy wine with a merry heart; for God now accepteth thy works. Let thy garments be always white; and let thy head lack no ointment. Live joyfully with the wife whom thou lovest all the days of the life of thy vanity, which he hath given thee under the sun, all the days of thy vanity: for that is thy portion in this life, and in thy labour which thou takest under the sun.

The visitation of God in the Garden of Eden with Adam and Ever after their fall is a prime example of different priorities in a relationship. Both Adam and Eve now realized they had lost God's friendship. "Then the man and his wife heard the sound of the Lord God as he was walking in the garden in the cool of the day, and they hid from the Lord God among the trees of the garden" (Genesis 3:8 NIV). God called to them, "Where are you?" and they answered, "We heard your voice in the garden, and we were afraid because we were naked; so we hid." God then said, "Who told you that you were naked? Have you eaten from the tree that I commanded you not to eat from?" The man said, "The woman you put here with me—she gave me some fruit from the tree, and I ate it" (Genesis 3:11–12 NIV).

Adam did not respond the same way that he had responded before eating the fruit. Prior to the fall, Adam described Eve thus: "This is now bone of my bones and flesh of my flesh; she shall be called 'woman,' for she was taken out of man" (Genesis 2:23). After the fall, he called her "the woman you put here" (Genesis 3:9). Accepting responsibility is part of work-life balance. "We all came into this world the same: naked, scared, and ignorant. After that, the life we end up with is simply an accumulation of all the choices we make" (Hardy 2010, 23). Yet Adam absolved himself of all responsibility for what had taken place in the garden.

Initially, in the Garden of Eden, after God created Adam and Eve, He gave them permission to eat from every tree in the garden except from the one in the center. He specifically told them that eating fruit from that tree would result in death (Genesis 2:15). The story of Adam and Eve in the Garden of Eden is all about the choices they made. They chose to eat of the fruit that God had told them not to eat, and as a result, they suffered the consequences. A consequence is defined as "something that happens as a result of a particular action or set of conditions" (*Merriam-Webster's* 2016, 296). This means that every individual has the opportunity to make choices but also must face the consequences of any particular action.

Choice is a very important aspect in life. Generally, life depends on the choices we make in the present that will impact our future. The choice that Adam and Eve made in the garden exacted a price that all humankind had to pay. Thankfully, the Bible says, "For the wages of sin is death, but the gift of God is eternal life in Christ our Lord" (Romans 6:23 NIV).

When a couple decides to get married, they make a choice together. If they accept their responsibilities, their marriage will be successful, but if they don't, their marriage will be unsuccessful. After the wedding day, they must work to build their relationship in order to achieve success.

What is the compound effect, and how does it relate to marriage? According to Hardy, the compound effect is rooted in the most important decisions that shape a person's destiny. These include little, everyday decisions that lead a person either to the fulfillment of personal desires or to disaster. "The compound effect is the principle of reaping huge rewards from a series of small, smart choices" (Hardy 2010, 9). Many married couples don't realize that "seemingly insignificant steps completed consistently over time will create a radical difference" (Hardy 2010, 10).

After the marriage ceremony, it might be difficult initially for a newly founded family to spend much time together, but with consistency and commitment, it will happen. It is imperative that the couple plan to spend time together. It is similar to a business manager who works with a budget. He or she may work countless hours to achieve certain financial goals. Seemingly insignificant decisions do not immediately result in large profits; however, consistent, small gains on a daily and even monthly basis will eventually result in the achievement of the larger goals. No matter how hard life may be at the beginning of a marriage, spending time together, even in small ways, is the key to success.

According to Hardy (2010, 23), everything in life exists because someone first made a choice about it. Choices are the foundation of every action. Family work-life balance is a choice and a commitment that a married couple must work on together in order to achieve success. True, lasting success requires a great deal of hard work (Hardy, 19). One of the biggest differences between a successful family and an unsuccessful one is that successful people in general are willing to do what unsuccessful people are not likely to do. Having a good marriage is not automatic. Try not to be the married couple who goes along with what they believe others would do (Hardy, 8). It is important that each married couple make decisions that will meet their needs. In life, everyone has their own preferences. What works for one couple may not necessarily work for another. But in building a strong family, spending time together is a must.

Family Work-Life Balance Equals Success

"It is possible to achieve success in life while at the same time maintaining balance between the personal and the professional" (Butterworth 2006, 17). Times have changed tremendously. There was a time when most families regularly ate meals together, sat together in worship services in church, and attended the funerals of departed friends together (Chapman 2003, 98). Nowadays, it is almost impossible for some families to spend much time together because they are too busy or their schedules don't permit such luxuries.

According to the Bible, "The days of our years are threescore years and ten; and if by reason of strength they be fourscore years, yet is their strength labour and sorrow; for it is soon cut off, and we fly away" (Psalm 90:10 KJV). This means that everyone has a time to live and a time to die; therefore, time management is critical. Everyone must manage their time according to their priorities. The Lord has said, "My Spirit will not contend with humans forever, for they are mortal; their days will be a hundred and twenty years" (Genesis 6:3 NIV). We are all responsible for doing all we are supposed to do during our allotted time frame. "To everything there is a season, and a time to every purpose under the heaven" (Ecclesiastes 3:1 KJV). This includes family time.

The first goal of the ultimate Christian life is to have a good relationship with God, then with family, and finally with friends. God designed the marriage relationship, followed by the parent-child relationship, as the most intimate relationship on earth. We should, therefore, never pursue activities that have little to do with building marriage and family relationships (Chapman 2003, 99). Furthermore,

Often the buzz phrase *quality time* engenders thoughts of excessive expectations that are difficult to meet. For example, quality time for parents means concentrated, uninterrupted time to spend with their children. It is believed that this time should make up in quality for the amount of time missed throughout the week (Witmer). Honestly, quality time is just that: any time that a person spends with his or her family. The whole family does not need to be present every time. For example, a father helping his son with his homework or taking his daughter shopping would constitute quality time (Witmer).

According to Driscoll and Driscoll (2012, 33), a husband and his wife should spend quality time together and learn to have extended and more intimate conversations. A good husband will go further by asking his wife how she is doing and how her day has been. He should listen without being distracted by phone calls or any other technology. It is insulting to his wife if he allows his cell phone to interrupt quality time during nonemergencies. Instead, couples should focus on each other. Try looking each other in the eye for extended periods of time, and draw from each other emotionally. Keep the advice to a minimum, and learn to listen, empathize, comfort, and encourage. Resist the constant urge to identify a problem and fix it.

"Successful people aren't necessarily more intelligent or more talented than anyone else. But their habits take them in the direction of becoming more informed, more knowledgeable, more competent, better skilled and better prepared" (Hardy 2010, 58). What is a habit? A habit is "something that a person does often in a regular and repeated way" (*Merriam-Webster's* 2016). According to Jack Canfield (2000, 6), "Your habits will determine your future." Choices are only meaningful when they are connected to our desires and dreams (Hardy 2010). In marriage, couples need to understand the choices they are making. Without a clear game plan, they will never achieve their goals.

Once we define what we are looking for, we can bring it to the table (Hardy 2010, 71). According to Hardy, "It takes three hundred instances of positive reinforcement to turn a new habit into unconscious practice" (85). One key to success is staying aware. If we really want to maintain a good habit, we must pay attention to it at least once a day (85). Furthermore, the simple way to develop a good habit is to stay on top of it by building on it with discipline (101). Successful people tend to become more successful: the rich get richer, and the happy get happier because they have learned the secret to maintaining a positive habit (97).

In order to be successful in marriage, couples must develop discipline, routines, and consistency in order to create momentum (Hardy 2010, 97). What is a routine? *Merriam-Webster's* (2016) defines it like this: "a sequence of actions regularly followed; a fixed program." A routine is something one does every day so that eventually it becomes automatic. In order to reach new goals and develop new habits, it is necessary to create new routines to support the new objectives (Hardy 2010, 99).

One trait that both those who fail and those who succeed in marriage have in common is a dislike of redundancy, but successful marriage partners persevere anyway. Everyone agrees that change is hard. That's why many people do not transform their bad habits and why many people end up unhappy and unhealthy (Hardy 2010, 90). Adopting any change requires practice. We can start by taking one small step, one action at a time. Progress may be very slow, but once a newly formed habit has kicked in, success and results compound rapidly (95).

Love is an emotion that everyone wants more of, and the best way to receive love is to give love. The goal in a marriage is to deepen the love and intimacy felt by each spouse. For instance, each morning a husband can plan some things that will make his wife feel loved, respected, and beautiful (Hardy 2010, 103). Spending time together as a family is an expression of love, and couples should always strive to maintain a healthy relationship by prioritizing family time (103). There are many important aspects of life, but spending time together as a family is one of the most important ones.

Married couples may glowingly boast to others about the importance of their family, but do they live as though family is important? Both men and women long for paradigms that will help them achieve greater balance. We all know that priorities are important, but how do we achieve those priorities? Commitment is the key.

According to Jack Canfield (2000, 229), "All broken relationships can be traced back to broken agreements. This includes business deals, marriages, family situations, your banker, friends, and any other flawed relationship between two or more people." Some men do not spend enough quality time with their children, and even when they are home, they are often distracted by thoughts of what they need to accomplish during the workday. Married couples must realize that their highest priority is family relationships, and they must unashamedly confess that their families are of utmost importance. When they neglect their families, they are neglecting their priorities (Butterworth 2006, 31).

What is integrity? Integrity is defined as "the quality or state of being complete; unbroken condition; wholeness; entirety" (*Webster's New World Dictionary* 2016). According to Jack Canfield (2000, 223), there is a simple and effective three-part formula to help all of us live with the utmost integrity. First, if we always tell the truth, people will in turn always trust us. Second, if we do what we say we will do, people will respect us. Finally, if we make others feel special, others will like us.

Every individual is responsible for their own marriage and life. Everyone is responsible for the choices they make and the actions they take. Everyone must also realize that "choices, behaviors, and habits are influenced by very powerful external forces" (Hardy 2010, 121). External forces are "pressures that arise from outside a system" (*Oxford English Dictionary* 1971). In the context of a business, external forces typically refer to those factors that render effect on the business and its market prices. In similar fashion, external forces have the power to affect a marriage or relationship.

In today's competitive society, most people consider work-life balance as important. Everyone is looking for perfect balance in life as the key to healthy living. According to Jack Canfield (2000, 65), there are two major pains in life. One is the pain of discipline; the other is the pain of regret. Discipline weighs ounces, but regret weighs tons when someone allows their dreams to drift along unfulfilled. No one wants to look back years later and say, "If only I had taken that business opportunity; now I would be further along in my life, and I could be doing better things for me and my family." "If only I had saved and invested regularly, now I would have my own company, and I would have a lot of money in the bank to enjoy life." "If only I had spent more time with my family, my children and I would have a better relationship." "If only I had taken care of my health, now I would be very healthy." Regret is a feeling of sadness about something, someone, or a path we took. For example, someone might regret leaving school too soon instead of finishing their degree. Regret, however, has no place in a thriving relationship built on the seven principles of a successful marriage.

I left school at 16, but I've had a great life, and I have no regrets.

Conclusion

This manuscript talks about the seven principles of a successful marriage—trust, faithfulness, fidelity, sex, forgiveness, respect, and love—and about how to accomplish a successful marriage. Married couples must understand that the wedding day is not the most important day in their marriage, even though it marks the beginning of their new life. According to Driscoll and Driscoll (2012, 207), the most important day in a marriage is the last day, because that is the day that really counts.

There is a reason the Bible says a man should leave his parents and attach to his wife, and they shall become one flesh (Genesis 2:18). Death is intended as the only power to separate a marriage. Therefore, the last day, the burial day, should not be filled with regret. On the contrary, the last day should be a day to rejoice and celebrate the life that once was shared. In marriage, and in all of life, the last day is the most important day. We would do well to remember the words of Revelation 3:11 (KJV): "Behold, I come quickly: hold that fast which thou hast, that no man take thy crown."

Theory without practice is the same as learning without execution. If someone gets married today and divorces tomorrow, it would have been preferable not to get married at all. I didn't do this research and write *The Seven Principles of a Successful Marriage* for myself. Instead, I wrote it to give married couples a clear understanding of how to have a successful marriage. It is intended to make a positive difference in the lives of all those who read it.

As I said in the introduction, I was motivated by my own parents' relationship, observing the way they lived according to the Scriptures. Throughout the years, I have learned many great tips from them and have incorporated them into my marriage. As a married man, I have realized that my wife is the greatest gift I have ever received from God. A gift of a wife is a gift of a lifetime.

According to Michael Pearl (2012, 21), Adam observed the animals relating to one another, yet he found no suitable counterpart for himself. Genesis explains that Adam did not find "a suitable helper" (Genesis 2:20). He recognized that something was missing, but he did not know what it was. It was in Adam's nature to need his yet-uncreated counterpart (21).

The common assumption is that Adam was naming all of the animals and realized that all of them had companions. The male had a female companion, and the female had a male companion. However, none of these were suitable companions for Adam, and because of this, he became sad and lonely.

God, recognizing Adam's loneliness, put him to sleep and fashioned Eve from one of his ribs. The Bible teaches that Eve was made for Adam (1 Corinthians 11:8). She was to be a companion and helper to him (Genesis 2:18). None of the previously created animals was suitable (Genesis 2:20). Adam was very happy to see that with Eve, he now had someone to talk to. This indicates that he was, in fact, waiting for such a companion (Genesis 2:23). Adam was pleased and said, "This is now bone of my bones and flesh of my flesh; she shall be called 'woman,' for she was taken out of man" (Genesis 2:23).

Before the creation of the woman, we can hypothesize that Adam may have grown introspective and sullen. Small droplets may have collected in the corners of his eyes, making the world foggy and intensifying his loneliness. The only thing that brought a smile to his face was the early morning walks with God. His devotion with God, until the sun first filtered through the forest and the animals drowsily opened their eyes, the man spoke his mind. Genesis observes that Adam did not find a help meet for him (Genesis 2:20). "Not found" indicates that he looked for his resemblance among the animals, intuitively knowing that he lacked something.

When a man and a woman fall in love, it is clear to them that they are made for each other. Men and women are meant to complement each other. "So God created man in his own image, in the image of God he created him; male and female he created them" (Genesis 1:27). To complement is to complete or bring something to perfection.

When the Bible says that two become one flesh, it insinuates that the one is only a half. Half is incomplete. For example, it takes both a male and a female to produce a baby. While men and women share many similarities, they are also very different. These differences provide wonderful opportunities for love and wholeness, but they can also pose the possibility of misunderstanding in regard to marriage.

Many perceived differences between men and women are generalizations. They are not judgments, so they require us to make categorical decisions. Fortunately, the general differences between the sexes help men and women to be better marriage partners. One such difference is contained in the story of God's original plan for marriage. God made man to be the provider, and He made woman to be the encourager. Adam was to cultivate the Garden of Eden, while Eve was to be a suitable helper who would encourage him and stand by his side (Genesis 3:16). This means that man is the protector, and the woman is the nurturer: "Unto the woman God said, I will greatly multiply thy sorrow and thy conception; in sorrow thou shall bring forth children; and thy desire shall be to thy husband, and he shall rule over you" (Genesis 2:16 KJV).

In a marriage, the husband is to be in charge, and the wife is to bring forth and nurture the next generation. Naturally, the man is to lead, guide, and protect. For these reasons, God made the man physically stronger than his female counterpart. On the other hand, God made the woman to be soft, gentle, and tender because she is the life giver. These fundamental differences are bred into the nature of both men and women.

The apostle Peter said that the woman is the weaker vessel: "Likewise, ye husbands, dwell with them according to knowledge, giving honour unto the wife, as unto the weaker vessel" (1 Peter 3:7 KJV). Human biology dictates that a combination of XY chromosomes creates a boy, and a combination of XX chromosomes creates a girl. This demonstrates that God planned differences between both men and women before they were created (*Human Body* 2008, 475). "The sex chromosomes are designated X and Y. A female has two X chromosomes, and a male one X chromosome and one Y chromosome. Because only the male has the Y chromosome, the father determines the sex of the child" (*Human Body* 2008, 475).

Many men enter marriage assuming that the sexual needs of their wives are the same as theirs. They believe sex will now be easy, convenient, and frequent. After all, who would turn down morally acceptable sex? However, during the honeymoon, they may encounter different sexual expectations from their mates, and things may change. Many men go through a period, often of many years, of quiet confusion, feelings of rejection, and ongoing frustration because their wives do not respond to their sexual desires as they expected. Out of this frustration come blaming, accusation, and bargaining. This moves couples further apart from each other. Nonetheless, God created marriage in order for men and women to be happy. Since it was instituted by God, the creator of the universe, marriage permits spouses to enjoy sexual intimacy and allows human beings to multiply and fill the earth with God's children (Genesis 22:14).

God will never forsake anyone, especially those who trust Him. According to the book of Genesis, *Jehovah-Jireh* means "God provides" (Genesis 22:8). It was also the name of a place in the land of Moriah. According to Genesis 22:5, God commanded Abraham to offer his son Isaac as a sacrifice (Genesis 22:5–8). After Isaac was bound and placed on an altar, the angel of the Lord stopped Abraham at the last minute, saying, "Now I know you fear God" (Genesis 22:12). At this point, Abraham saw a ram caught in some nearby bushes and sacrificed the ram instead of Isaac (Genesis 22:5, 8). Likewise, God will provide for married couples who trust in Him.

Lastly, the Scriptures say, "But seek first the kingdom of God and His righteousness, and all these things shall be added to you" (Matthew 6:33). What is the kingdom of God? The apostle Paul tells us in Romans 14:17 that the kingdom of God is not eating and drinking but "righteousness and peace and joy in the Holy Spirit."

Couples should welcome Jesus into their lives if they want to have successful marriages. When a man and a woman decide to get married, it is very important that they invite Jesus to the wedding before planning anything else. Jesus should always be the first guest invited to a Christian wedding. The Scriptures say that Jesus was invited to a wedding in Cana of Galilee, where the wine ran out in the middle of the reception (John 2:1–11). Jesus performed His first miracle right there, providing six jars of wine for the occasion. "The master of the banquet tasted the water that had been turned into wine. He did not realize where it had come from, though the servants who had drawn the water knew" (John 2:9). God is a provider for His people.

When spouses trust in God, they are much more likely to enjoy a pleasant marriage. Marriage is good, and something most people desire. Single people have the right to get married and create a family. They should not allow fear to come between them and their futures; if they allow fear into their lives, they may become paranoid by all the negative stories they have heard about marriage. Such fearful, suspicious people are under bondage and do not know how to accept or receive the favor of the Lord. They miss the truth of Proverbs 18:22 (KJV): "Whoso findeth a wife findeth a good thing, and obtaineth favor of the Lord."

Worry and fear of change demonstrate a lack of trust in God. Sadly, we all tend to worry about things we have no control over or power to change. However, if individuals are able to trust God, they will no longer be plagued by worry and apprehension. God is the greatest decision-maker of all time, especially for those who trust in Him.

The book of Genesis is all about beginnings. It is the book of the beginning of life, marriage, truth, and hope. Some may believe that marriage is too old-fashioned. Others may say the stories of the Bible are too old or irrelevant. However, we must go back to the beginning in order to enjoy everything that God has in store for us. Marriage is one of the first and oldest institutions that God created. It must be respected and restored the way God intended it to be.

Sex is a glorious gift from God that brings great joy to both men and women when it is expressed in the right way. A man is never satisfied with sex until he is a master at pleasing his wife (Pearl 2012, 61). At the same time, sex can also derail lives when it is abused. For example, the apostle Paul instructed the Christians at Corinth to deliver a sinful brother "unto Satan for the destruction of the flesh" (1 Corinthians 5:5 NIV). This sounds like a very severe requirement, but the apostle was dealing with a gross example of immorality in the Corinthian church. A man had become sexually intimate with his stepmother (the language is very precise: his "father's wife," as opposed to his own mother). The church members were not offended by the sordid situation; rather, they glorified it. However, the apostle called for retribution by delivering the offending brother to Satan for "the destruction of the flesh."

Salvation is God's gift in response to the problem of sin in humanity and all of creation. The good news of salvation is that God has acted to reverse the tide of sin, which has broken human relationships with God, others, and the created world. The fact of sin, or evil, in the world has two main consequences in human affairs. First, it renders people guilty. Sin means that people do not worship God as their loving Creator but instead choose their own way and place other things ahead of God. This deep offense against God is at the same time a deep offense against themselves, and it results in offenses against others. People stand guilty, in need of forgiveness and restoration to God and their own true nature.

It is equally important to know that a good marriage is the primary place where a man receives acceptance and grace. When a man has a wife who loves him and takes him into the most intimate of embraces, he receives a powerful symbol of pure love that transcends merit. Great sex is not just about having one's desires fulfilled. It also means giving of oneself, receiving love, and meeting the needs of another. "Adam needed sex, but that is a small need compared to the need to have a soul mate" (Pearl 2012, 21).

The time has come for the decision-makers to move toward God. The kingdom of God is near. According to Mark 1:15, "The time is fulfilled, and the kingdom of God is at hand: repent you, and believe the gospel." Spouses must believe in themselves as well as in each other. In addition, couples must seek God in prayer because prayer is the key to success. As Paul said, "Rejoice always, pray without ceasing, and give thanks in all circumstances; for this is the will of God in Christ Jesus for you" (1 Thessalonians 5:16–18 ESV). Believe it or not, having a successful marriage requires a lot of prayer. Prayer is a great tool for anyone who wishes to have a successful marriage.

Reference List

Alston, K. 1991. "Teaching, Philosophy, and Eros: Love as a Relation to Truth." *Educational Theory*, 41 (4): 385–95.

Amato, P. R., and J. G. Gilbreth. 1999. "Nonresident Fathers and Children's Well-Being: A Meta-Analysis." *Journal of Marriage and the Family*, 557–573.

American Bar Association Standing Committee on the Delivery of Legal Services. 1994. *Responding to the Needs of the Self-Represented Divorce Litigant*. Chicago, IL: American Bar Association.

Axinn, W. G., and A. Thornton. 2000. "The Transformation in the Meaning of Marriage." In *The Ties That Bind: Perspectives on Marriage and Cohabitation*, edited by L. J. Waite. New York, NY: Walter de Gruyter.

Bell, J. S. 2010. *Love Is a Flame: Stories of What Happens When Love Is Rekindled*. South Bloomington, MN: Bethany House.

Bengtson, V. L. 2001. "Beyond the Nuclear Family: The Increasing Importance of Multigenerational Bonds." *Journal of Marriage and Family*, 63 (1): 1–16.

Bienvenu, M. J. Sr. 1970. "Measurement of Marital Communication." *Family Coordinator*, 26–31.

Bierly, P. E. III, E. H. Kessler, and E. W. Christensen. 2000. "Organizational Learning, Knowledge and Wisdom." *Journal of Organizational Change Management*, 13 (6): 595–618.

Bland, R., and Y. Darlington. 2002. "The Nature and Sources of Hope: Perspectives of Family Caregivers of People with Serious Mental Illness." *Perspectives in Psychiatric Care*, 38 (2): 61–68.

Blossfeld, H. P., and J. Huinink. 1991. "Human Capital Investments or Norms of Role Transition? How Women's Schooling and Career Affect the Process of Family Formation." *American Journal of Sociology*, 143–68.

Boshart, D. 2003. *Sex and Faith: Celebrating God's Gifts*. Harrisonburg, VA: Faith and Life Resources.

Brown, E. M. 2001. *Patterns of Infidelity and Their Treatment*. Philadelphia, PA: Brunner-Routledge.

Burgess, E. W., and H. J. Locke. 1945. *The Family: From Institution to Companionship*. Oxford, England: American Book.

Burleson, B. R., and W. H. Denton. 1997. "The Relationship Between Communication Skill and Marital Satisfaction: Some Moderating Effects." *Journal of Marriage and the Family*, 884–902.

Chapman, G. 2003. *Covenant Marriage: Building Communication and Intimacy*. Nashville, TN: Broadman & Holman.

Chapman, G. 2010. *The 5 Love Languages: The Secret to Love That Lasts*. Chicago, IL: Northfield.

Chapman, G., and J. S. Bell. 2011. *Love Is a Verb Devotional: 365 Daily Inspirations to Bring Love Alive*. Grand Rapids, MI: Baker.

Cole, G. A. 2009. *God the Peacemaker: How Atonement Brings Shalom*. Downers Grove, IL: Apollos/InterVarsity.

Comanor, W. S., and L. Phillips. 2002. "The Impact of Income and Family Structure on Delinquency." *Journal of Applied Economics*, 5 (2), 209–32.

Connelly, D. 2005. *Forgiveness: Making Peace with the Past*. Downers Grove, IL: InterVarsity.

Copen, C., K. Daniels, J. Vespa, and W. D. Mosher. 2012. "First Marriages in the United States: Data from the 2006–2010 National Survey of Family Growth." *National Health Statistics Reports*, 49, 1–21.

Curran, D. J., and C. M. Renzetti. 2000. *Social Problems: Society in Crisis*. Boston, MA: Allyn and Bacon.

Curran, D. J., and C. M. Renzetti. 2007. *Theories of Crime*, 3rd ed. Boston, MA: Allyn and Bacon.

Davis, J. H. 2014. *United States of America—Right Now: Distortion of the Dream*. Bloomington, IN: Xlibris.

Dillon, R. S. 2001. "Self-Forgiveness and Self-Respect." *Ethics*, 112 (1): 53–83.

Driscoll, M., and Driscoll, G. 2012. *Real Marriage: The Truth About Sex, Friendship, and Life Together*. Nashville, TN: Thomas Nelson.

Eggerichs, E. 2004. *Love Respect: The Love She Most Desires, the Respect He Desperately Needs*. Nashville, TN: Integrity.

Elliott, B. J., and M. P. M. Richards. 1991. "Children and Divorce: Educational Performance and Behavior Before and After Parental Separation." *International Journal of Law, Policy, and the Family*, 5 (3): 258.

Emmons, R. A., and C. A. Crumpler. 2000. "Gratitude as a Human Strength: Appraising the Evidence." *Journal of Social and Clinical Psychology*, 19 (1): 56–69.

Enright, R. D., P. Conroy, S. Freedman, J. H. Hebl, Y. Park, I. Sarinopoulos, . . . and K. Pierce. 1991. "The Moral Development of Forgiveness." In *Handbook of Moral Behavior and Development*, edited by W. M. Kurtines and J. L. Gewirtz 1, 123–52. Hillsdale, NJ: Lawrence Erlbaum Associates.

Evans, T. 2010. *For Married Women Only: Three Principles for Honoring Your Husband*. Chicago, IL: Moody.

Farrel, P. 2011. *52 Ways to Wow Your Husband: How to Put a Smile on His Face*. Eugene, OR: Harvest House.

Ferraro, K. F. 1995. *Fear of Crime: Interpreting Victimization Risk*. Albany, NY: SUNY Press.

Ferrebe, L. A. 2001. *The Healthy Marriage Handbook*. Nashville, TN: Broadman & Holman.

Fincham, F. D., F. Paleari, and C. Regalia. 2002. "Forgiveness in Marriage: The Role of Relationship Quality, Attributions, and Empathy." *Personal Relationships*, 9 (1): 27–37.

Fitzpatrick, M. A., and L. D. Ritchie. 1994. "Communication Schemata Within the Family." *Human Communication Research*, 20 (3): 275–301.

Flanagan, C. 2003. "Trust, Identity, and Civic Hope." *Applied Developmental Science*, 7 (3): 165–71.

Freedman, S. 1998. "Forgiveness and Reconciliation: The Importance of Understanding How They Differ." *Counseling and Values*, 42 (3): 200.

Galvin, K. M. 2008. *Family Communication: Cohesion and Change.* New York, NY: Taylor & Francis.

Geisler, N. L. 2010. *Christian Ethics: Contemporary Issues and Options.* Grand Rapids, MI: Baker Academic.

Gertzen, G. 2014. "Endure Hardship: Suffering in the Ministry, Expectations of Pastoral Trainees in the Reformed Evangelical Anglican Church of South Africa." MA thesis. South African Theological Seminary.

Giddens, A. 2013. *The Transformation of Intimacy: Sexuality, Love and Eroticism in Modern Societies.* Cambridge, UK: Polity.

Goodman, J. F. 2009. "Respect-Due and Respect-Earned: Negotiating Student-Teacher Relationships." *Ethics and Education*, 4 (1): 3–17.

Gordon, M. T., and S. Riger. 1991. *The Female Fear: The Social Cost of Rape.* Chicago, IL: University of Illinois Press.

Grant, C. 1996. "For the Love of God: Agape." *The Journal of Religious Ethics*, 3–21.

Groom, N. 1991. *From Bondage to Bonding: Escaping Codependency, Embracing Biblical Love.* Colorado Springs, CO: NavPress.

Groom, N. 2000. *Risking Intimacy: Overcoming Fear, Finding Rest.* Grand Rapids, MI: Baker.

Grunebaum, M. G., I. Hurwitz, N. M. Prentice, and B. M. Sperry. 1962. "Fathers of Sons with Primary Neurotic Learning Inhibitions." *American Journal of Orthopsychiatry*, 32 (3): 462.

Grunseth, J., and B. Grunseth. 2011. *I'm Getting Married! Preparing Your Heart for a Lifetime.* Orlando, FL: New Life Resources.

Harbaugh, W. T. 1998. "The Prestige Motive for Making Charitable Transfers." *American Economic Review*, 277–82.

Harley, W. F. 2006. *I Promise You: Preparing for a Marriage That will Last a Lifetime*. Grand Rapids, MI: Revell.

Harley, W. F. 2011. *His Needs, Her Needs: Building an Affair-Proof Marriage*. Grand Rapids, MI: Revell.

Hawley, D. R., and L. DeHaan. 1996. "Toward a Definition of Family Resilience: Integrating Life-Span and Family Perspectives." *Family Process*, 35 (3): 283–98.

Hoover-Dempsey, K. V., and H. M. Sandler. 1997. "Why Do Parents Become Involved in Their Children's Education?" *Review of Educational Research*, 67 (1): 3–42.

Jacquet, S. E., and C. A. Surra. 2001. "Parental Divorce and Premarital Couples: Commitment and Other Relationship Characteristics." *Journal of Marriage and Family*, 63 (3): 627–38.

Johnson-Medland, N. T. 2011. *Feed My Sheep, Lead My Sheep: A Handbook of Leadership Formation for Individuals and Groups*. Eugene, OR: Resource.

Joseph, C. 2013. *Women Living Well: Finding Your Joy in God, Your Man, Your Kids, and Your Home*. Nashville, TN: Thomas Nelson.

Kendall, J., and D. Jones. 2005. *Lady in Waiting: Becoming God's Best While Waiting for Mr. Right*, expanded edition. Shippensburg, PA: Destiny Image.

Kendall, R. T. 2002. *Total Forgiveness: True Inner Peace Awaits You!* Lake Mary, FL: Charisma House.

Kirschner, D. 2011. *Sealing the Deal: The Love Mentor's Guide to Lasting Love*. New York, NY: Center Street.

Konstan, D. 2013. "Eros and Narrative in the Novel." *Greek Fiction*, 49.

Ladd, G. E. 1993. *A Theology of the New Testament*. Grand Rapids, MI: Wm. B. Eerdmans.

Laumann-Billings, L., and R. E. Emery. 2000. "Distress Among Young Adults from Divorced Families." *Journal of Family Psychology*, 14 (4), 671.

Larzelere, R. E., and T. L. Huston. 1980. "The Dyadic Trust Scale: Toward Understanding Interpersonal Trust in Close Relationships." *Journal of Marriage and the Family*, 595–604.

Lawrence, B. 2004. *The Practice of the Presence of God*. Peabody, MA: Hendrickson.

Luxton, M. 1980. *More Than a Labour of Love: Three Generations of Women's Work in the Home*. Toronto, ON: Women's Press.

Mace, D. 1987. "Three Ways of Helping Married Couples." *Journal of Marital and Family Therapy*, 13 (2), 179–85.

Mack, D., and Blankenhorn, D., eds. 2001. *The Book of Marriage: The Wisest Answers to the Toughest Questions*. Grand Rapids, MI: Eerdmans.

Martin, A. M. 2008. "Exploring Forgiveness: The Relationship Between Feeling Forgiven by God and Self-Forgiveness for an Interpersonal Offense." Dissertation. Cleveland, OH: Case Western Reserve University.

Martin, W. C. 1964. *The Layman's Bible Encyclopedia*. Nashville, TN: Southwestern.

Matheson, K. W. 2009. "Fidelity in Marriage: It's More Than You Think." The Church of Jesus Christ of Latter-Day Saints. Retrieved from LDS.org.

May, S. M. 2007. *How to Argue So Your Spouse Will Listen: 6 Principles for Turning Arguments into Conversations.* Nashville, TN: Thomas Nelson.

McCullough, M. E., S. J. Sandage, and E. L. Worthington. 1997. *To Forgive Is Human: How to Put Your Past in the Past.* Downers Grove, IL: InterVarsity.

Nelson's Minister's Manual. Nashville, TN: Thomas Nelson.

North, J. 1987. "Wrongdoing and Forgiveness." *Philosophy*, 62 (242), 499–508.

Omartian, S. 2001. *The Power of a Praying Husband.* Eugene, OR: Harvest House.

Omartian, S. 2009. *The Power of Prayer to Change Your Marriage.* Eugene, OR: Harvest House.

Ortlund, A. 1985. *Building a Great Marriage.* Old Tappan, NJ: F. H. Revell.

Owen, W. F. 1984. "Interpretive Themes in Relational Communication." *Quarterly Journal of Speech*, 70 (3), 274–87.

Pangle, L. S. 2003. *Aristotle and the Philosophy of Friendship.* Cambridge, U.K.: Cambridge University Press.

Pearl, D. 2010. *Preparing to Be a Help Meet.* Pleasantville, TN: No Greater Joy Ministries.

Pearl, M. 2012. *Created to Need a Help Meet: A Marriage Guide for Men.* Pleasantville, TN: No Greater Joy Ministries.

Peters, B. J. 2009. *The Gift of a Lifetime: Building a Marriage That Lasts*. Bloomington, IN: AuthorHouse.

Ponton, L. 2007. "What Is Forgiveness?" *Psych Central*. Retrieved from https://psychcentral.com/lib/what-is-forgiveness/.

Popenoe, D. 1993. "American Family Decline, 1960–1990: A Review and Appraisal." *Journal of Marriage and the Family*, 527–42.

Post, S. G. 1991. "Conditional and Unconditional Love." *Modern Theology*, 7 (5): 435–46.

Prager, K. 1997. *The Psychology of Intimacy*. New York, NY: Guilford.

Rainey, D., ed. 2010. *Preparing for Marriage: Discover God's Plan for a Lifetime of love*. Ventura, CA: Gospel Light.

Rainey, D., and B. Rainey. 2000. *Starting Your Marriage Right: What You Need to Know and Do in the Early Years to Make It Last a Lifetime*. Nashville, TN: Thomas Nelson.

Regan, P. C., and E. Berscheid. 1999. *Lust: What We Know About Human Sexual Desire*. Thousand Oaks, CA: Sage.

Renner, R. 2003. *Sparkling Gems from the Greek: 365 Greek Word Studies for Every Day of the Year to Sharpen Your Understanding of God's Word*. Tulsa, OK: Teach All Nations.

Richmond, R. L. 2004. *Anger and Forgiveness*. Cincinnati, OH: Trade Mark Publishing.

Rogers, E. M. 1973. *Communication Strategies for Family Planning*. New York, NY: Free Press.

Rye, M. S., K. I. Pargament, A. M. Amir, G. L. Beck, E. N. Dorff, . . . and C. Hallisey. 2000. "Religious Perspectives on Forgiveness." *Forgiveness: Theory, Research, and Practice*, 17–40.

Sanderlin, D. 2010. *The Christian Way to Be Happily Married*. San Diego, CA: Christian Starlight.

Schaefer, M. T., and D. H. Olson. 1981. "Assessing Intimacy: The Pair Inventory." *Journal of Marital and Family Therapy*, 7 (1): 47–60.

Schnarch, D. 2002. *Passionate Marriage: Keeping Love and Intimacy Alive in Committed Relationships*. Evergreen, CO: Marriage and Family Health Center.

Seebran, S. 1999. *How to Handle Loneliness*. Columbus, GA: Brentwood Christian.

Smalley, G., and E. Smalley. 2015. *Ready to Wed: 12 Ways to Start a Marriage You'll Love*. Carol Stream, IL: Tyndale.

Sowing Circle. 2015. *The Blue Letter Bible*. Retrieved from www.blueletterbible.org.

Stanley, S. M., H. J. Markman, M. St. Peters, and B. D. Leber. 1995. "Strengthening Marriages and Preventing Divorce: New Directions in Prevention Research." *Family Relations*, 392–401.

Stephens, S. 2003. *20 (Surprisingly Simple) Rules and Tools for a Great Marriage*. Wheaton, IL: Tyndale.

Stevens, R. P. 1986. *Married for Good: The Lost Art of Staying Happily Married*. Downers Grove, IL: InterVarsity.

Stewart, A. L. 1998. "Covenant Marriage: Legislating Family Values." *Indiana Law Review*, 32:509.

Sullivan, P. L. 2005. "Culture, Divorce, and Family Mediation in Hong Kong." *Family Court Review*, 43 (1): 109–23.

Swaggart, J. 2006. *The Expositor's Study Bible* (Giant print King James Version edition). Baton Rouge, LA: Jimmy Swaggart Ministries.

Waite, L. J. 2005. "Marriage and Family." In *Handbook of Population*, edited by D. L. Poston and M. Micklin. New York, NY: Kluwer Academic/Plenum.

Waite, L. J., and M. Gallagher. 2001. *The Case for Marriage: Why Married People are Happier, Healthier and Better Off Financially*. New York, NY: Broadway.

Wallerstein, J. S. 1987. "Children of Divorce: Report of a Ten-Year Follow-Up of Early Latency-Age Children." *American Journal of Orthopsychiatry*, 57 (2): 199.

Warren, R. 2012. *The Purpose Driven Life: What on Earth Am I Here For?* Expanded edition. Grand Rapids, MI: Zondervan.

Warren, R., and J. Baker. 1998. *Celebrate Recovery*. Grand Rapids, MI: Zondervan.

Watkins, P. C., J. Uhder, A. Webber, S. Pichinevenskiy, and A. Sparrow. 2011. *Religious Affections: The Importance of Gratitude Toward God to Spiritual Well-Being*. Poster presented at the Annual Convention of the Association for Psychological Science, Washington, D.C.

Webster's New World College Dictionary. LoveToKnow Corp. 2016.. Web. April 17, 2016.

Weiss, Y., and R. J. Willis. 1985. "Children as Collective Goods and Divorce Settlements." *Journal of Labor Economics*, 268–92.

Welch, C. H. 1945. *The Eternal God Is Thy Refuge*. London: Berean Publishing Trust.

Wentland, J. J., and E. D. Reissing. 2011. "Taking Casual Sex Not Too Casually: Exploring Definitions of Casual Sexual Relationships." *The Canadian Journal of Human Sexuality*, 20 (3): 75–91.

Wiersbe, W. W. 1992. *Wiersbe's Expository Outlines on the New Testament*. Wheaton, IL: Victor Books.

Wiersbe, W. W. 2007. *The Wiersbe Bible Commentary: The Complete Old Testament in One Volume*. Colorado Springs, CO: Cook.

Willi, J. 1984. *Couples in Collusion: The Unconscious Dimension in Partner Relationships*. Claremont, CA: Hunter House.

Worthington, E. L., and F. DiBlasio. 1990. "Promoting Mutual Forgiveness Within the Fractured Relationship." *Psychotherapy: Theory, Research, Practice, Training*, 27 (2): 219.

Wright, H. N. 2012. *Communication: Key to Your Marriage: The Secret to True Happiness*. Ventura, CA: Regal.

Wright, H. N., and W. Roberts. 1997. *Before You Say "I Do": A Marriage Preparation Manual for Couples*. Irvine, CA: Harvest House.

Ziglar, Z. 1985. Published in Nashville, Tennessee, by Olivier-Nelson Books.

About the Author

Rev. Dr. Hilaire Louis Jean is the author of *The Seven Principles of a Successful Marriage* and the senior pastor and founder of Church of God Prince of Peace in Miami Florida. He graduated from Moody Bible Institute in Chicago, Illinois, and received a certificate for adult Bible studies. He graduated from Barry University with a bachelor of science in professional administration and then graduated with a bachelor of arts in theology from Life Christian University. He continued his education, obtaining a master of arts in theology and a doctor of ministry in theology, both from Life Christian University.

Dr. Hilaire Louis Jean is a servant of the Lord who has shown himself honorable, steadfast, and obedient to all that God has called him to accomplish. He is a great motivator with a tireless work ethic and possesses a loving, positive attitude that is infectious to those around him. He is a strong leader, a good listener, and a devoted and loving husband and father to his family. He is kind and compassionate, always available to help others, and offers great advice and direction. He is eager to excel and succeed in everything he does.

Dr. Hilaire Louis Jean has been called to preach the gospel of Jesus Christ, obeying the words of the apostle Paul: "Preach the word! Be ready in season and out of season. Convince, rebuke, exhort, with all longsuffering and teaching" (2 Timothy 4:2 KJV). The journey has not been easy, but the Lord has been faithful to draw him closer to Himself and prepare him to serve God and His people even more.

CPSIA information can be obtained
at www.ICGtesting.com
Printed in the USA
BVHW031521041122
651158BV00012B/1409

9 781959 165828